Paradisus Dei Prayer Handbook

TO FIND AND ADORE GOD WITHIN THE HOME

BY STEVE BOLLMAN

PARADISUS DEI

....

HELPING FAMILIES DISCOVER THE SUPERABUNDANCE OF GOD

A Publication of Paradisus Dei • www.paradisusdei.org

MORNING OFFERING

Dear Mother,
I consecrate myself and this day to you,
in the mystery of your Immaculate Conception, totus tuus.
Ease the doubts, the fears and the distractions of my mind.
Give me to drink of your desire;
and let your fiat be resplendent in my life.
Amen.

PARADISUS DEI'S PRAYER FOR THE NEW EVANGELIZATION

Heavenly Mother, Spotless Bride of the Spotless Lamb, Your children stand gathered together before you. With St. Joseph and the Apostle John we wish to bring you into our home, so that you may open to us the treasures of your Immaculate Heart. Reveal to us the hidden face of your Son, present in our midst.

Teach us to trust in the abundance of the Father's mercy. Make us docile to the voice of the Spirit echoing in our depths. Grant that the seeds of grace sown in us would not be lost, but blossom forth into life everlasting. Dawn of Salvation, Star of the New Evangelization Grant that the darkness may not prevail over the light.

Together with St. John Paul II, we consecrate ourselves to you in the mystery of your Immaculate Conception, Totus Tuus. Send us into the great mission field of the family, so that among all the nations, the praise of God may resound on the lips of infants and of babes. By the grace of God, in the Power of the Holy Spirit, help us to build a civilization worthy of the human person, created male and female, created in the image and likeness of the Triune God who is love.

Amen.

TABLE OF CONTENTS

The Mystery of the Holy Family. 4

The School of Nazareth and the Seven Steps. 9

The Spiritual Journey. 18

The Challenges and Support in the Spiritual Life 24

Building a Spiritual Plan of Life. 31

Our Lady and the New Springtime of Christianity. 43

The Most Holy Rosary of the Blessed Virgin Mary. 47

The Divine Mercy Chaplet. 68

How to Pray a Rosary 69

Daily Plan of Life 71

The Mystery of the Holy Family

．．※．．

"Jesus went down with Mary and Joseph and came to Nazareth ... and increased in wisdom and in stature, and in favor with God and man."
(Luke 2:51-52).

We shall never fully grasp the life of the Holy Family at Nazareth. It "was ... a paradise on earth, endless delights in this place of grief: it was a glory already begun in the vileness, abjection and lowliness of their life" *(Monsignor Jean Jacques Olier, 1608-1658)*. Indeed, the Paradise of Nazareth was greater than the Paradise in Eden.

In Eden, Adam and Eve heard "the sound of the Lord God walking in the garden" *(Genesis 2:8)*. In Nazareth, Mary and Joseph gazed into the eyes of Jesus Christ, the Word Incarnate. In Eden, Adam and Eve "hid themselves from the presence of the Lord God" *(Genesis 2:8)*. In Nazareth, Mary and Joseph remained one with God: "But standing by the cross of Jesus were his mother ..." *(John 19:25)*. But we must go much further.

God's presence in Nazareth was a Trinitarian reality. To be sure, only Jesus Christ was God Incarnate, but the entire Blessed Trinity dwelt in the home at Nazareth in a unique and unrepeatable way:

- Jesus Christ is the Word Incarnate: "And the Word became flesh and dwelt among us" *(John 1:14)*.
- Mary was "overshadowed" *(Luke 1:35)* by the Holy Spirit. She is human and only human, but her union with the Holy Spirit is so profound that it is "inexpressible" *(St. Maximillian Kolbe)*.
- St. Joseph was the shadow of the Father *(Cf. Luke 2:48)*. Jesus "conversed and communed visibly with God His Father, veiled under the person of St. Joseph, by whom His Father rendered Himself visible to Him" *(Monsignor Jean Jacques Olier, 1608-1658)*.

Unfortunately, the life of the Holy Family at Nazareth has remained inaccessible, shrouded by the thick cloud of Christ's hidden life ... until now. In the past two hundred years, Our Lady has formed great saints whom she granted access to the home at Nazareth. We will allow them to pull back its veil so that our homes may better reflect that hidden home at Nazareth and share in its joy.

St. Charles de Foucauld and the Presence of God

"I have glimpsed [the life of God] walking the streets of Nazareth."

St. Charles de Foucauld was born into a wealthy family in 1858 in Strasbourg, France. His parents died when he was five. He was adopted by his grandfather, who died when Charles was nineteen. Charles inherited a fortune—but his life spiraled downward. He abandoned the faith and indulged his passions. He joined the army, but his quarters were filled with the finest cooks ... and the prettiest "party girls." He was disciplined by the army on numerous occasions and placed on leave. His fortune was placed in the hands of a conservator when the courts declared him a "spendthrift." Charles needed a change.

He accepted a commission to the Sahara Desert. He fell in love with the vastness, silence and solitude of the desert. At great personal risk, he scouted the entire Sahara. When his reports were published, he became famous and returned to Paris. Despite the sudden fame, money and women, he longed for the silence and solitude of the desert.

He began a correspondence with a devout cousin, Marie de Bondy. She convinced him to see Fr. Huvelin at St. Augustin Church in Paris. Charles entered the confessional as an atheist and left as a man of God. He left the army and became a monk. His wanderings took him to Nazareth where, at last, he glimpsed the mystery he sought:

"Jesus came to Nazareth, the place of the hidden life, of ordinary life, of family life, of prayer, work, obscurity, silent virtues, practiced with no witnesses other than God, his friends and neighbors. Nazareth, the place where most people lead their lives" *(Charles de Foucauld, Essential Writings, p. 28).*

Charles came to understand that at Nazareth, Jesus didn't look or act like God. No miraculous cures or profound teachings. Christ was simply present in the normal events of everyday family life. It was this presence that transformed the home at Nazareth.

This is the mystery of your home. Christ is present in all the details of normal everyday life. He is hidden like at Nazareth, but he is there. Our challenge is to discover his presence and allow it to transform our lives.

St. John Bosco and the Path of Joy

"Let the boys ... jump, run and make as much noise as they please."

John Bosco was born in a small farming village outside Turin, Italy in 1815. His father died when he was two years old. John's older step-brother Antonio became the breadwinner of the family and had no appreciation for "book learning." He wanted laborers on the farm, but God had other plans for John, which were revealed to him in a dream.

"When he was nine years old, he had a dream ... in a field surrounded by a crowd of boys ... Some ... were fighting and using bad language ... he ... dashed in among them and laid about him with his fists ... and a battle royal began ... In the middle of this ruckus appeared a noble-looking Man ... 'Come here,' he said ... 'Be kind to them, lead them, teach them that sin is evil and that purity is a precious gift.' ... 'By listening to the woman I shall send to you, you will do everything with ease'" *(Lappin, P., Give Me Souls, Preface to Chapter 1).*

To fulfill this mission, Don Bosco became a priest and founded the second largest religious order in the Church (the Salesians of Don Bosco) with the mission to care for poor boys. He achieved "miraculous" results through his "preventive system" of education, which was "based on reason and religion, and above all on kindness." Don Bosco understood that Christ wants to share his joy with us: "That my joy may be in you, and that your joy may be full" *(John 15:11).*

As such, Don Bosco was fond of saying, "Let the boys have full liberty to jump, run and make as much noise as they please ... 'Do anything you like,' the great friend of youth, St. Philip [Neri] used to say, 'as long as you do not sin.'" Don Bosco exhausted himself bringing authentic joy to his boys.

The home at Nazareth was filled with joy. Your home is called to be filled with joy. Like Don Bosco, we must learn to adopt a spirit of joyful service to the members of our family. When we do, our homes will begin to look a bit more like the home at Nazareth.

St. Therese and Loving Sacrifice

"I do not regret having surrendered myself to love."

St. Therese was born into a devout family in Normandy, France. Her parents are the first couple to be canonized together as a couple. Like Therese, each of her four sisters entered religious life. Nonetheless, this idyllic setting knew much suffering. Therese lost her mother when she was just four years old. She developed a very special relationship to Our Lady, who miraculously cured Therese from a grave illness when Therese was ten.

Therese became a Carmelite nun at just fifteen. There she sought to live the life of Our Lady at Nazareth: "I know, O Mother full of grace, that you lived in great poverty in Nazareth ... no raptures, miracles or ecstasies lightened your life ... you chose to tread the everyday paths so as to show little ones the way to heaven." Therese ultimately discovered that this was the path of loving sacrifice in the smallest details of daily life.

"I understood it was Love alone that made the Church's members act ... that Love comprised all vocations, that love was everything, that it embraced all times and places ... Then in the excess of my delirious joy, I cried out: O Jesus, my Love ... my vocation, at last I have found it ... my vocation is Love."

Therese would learn to live this vocation to Love through her little way, practicing little virtues in the mundane things of everyday life ... but offering them with great love to God. Two years before the end of her short life of 24, she made the supreme sacrifice to God: "I offer myself as a victim of holocaust to your merciful love, asking You to consume me incessantly ... thus I may become a martyr of your Love, O my God." Therese's "little way of love" helped her to become the "greatest modern saint" *(Pope St. Pius X)*.

Loving sacrifice was at the very heart of the life of the Holy Family at Nazareth. Each member sacrificing all to God for the sake of the other. When we learn to live loving sacrifice like the Holy Family, then our homes will also become "a little Paradise on earth."

Pope St. John Paul II and the Importance of the Family

"One hand fired the gun. Another hand guided the bullet."

Karol Wojtyla was born into a devout family in Wadowice, Poland in 1920. Karol experienced painful loses early in life. His mother died when he was 8 and his older brother when Karol was 12. Karol was intellectually gifted and devout from his youth. He was the valedictorian of his high school class and an altar server at daily Mass.

During World War II he attended an underground seminary in Krakow. After the war, he quickly ascended the hierarchical ranks within the Church and attended the Second Vatican Council as one of the youngest bishops. On October 16, 1978, he was elected as the first non-Italian pope in almost five centuries. He entrusted his pontificate to Our Lady "*totus tuus*" (totally yours) and remained steadfastly devoted to her as he had been since his childhood.

He was convicted of the importance of the family in the divine plan of salvation: "The family is placed at the heart of the great struggle between good and evil, between life and death, between love and all that is opposed to love" *(Letter to Families, #24)*. He began his pontificate with a series of Wednesday audiences on the union between man and woman—now called the Theology of the Body. On his way to found The John Paul II Institute for Studies on Marriage and Family, an assassination attempt on his life occurred. He was saved by the intervention of Our Lady: "One hand fired the gun. Another hand guided the bullet."

He pointed to the Holy Family as the model of every family: "It is in the Holy Family ... that every Christian family must be reflected ... It is ... the prototype and example for all Christian families" *(Redemptoris Custos, #7)*. Outside of their home at Nazareth, the Holy Family experienced great struggle and pain. Within their home, they experienced love, peace and joy in the presence of God. This is the mystery of your home. Your family may have a share in the love, peace and joy of the Holy Family ... if you learn from them the way ... and follow their example.

The School of Nazareth and the Seven Steps

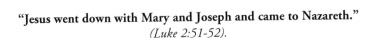

"Jesus went down with Mary and Joseph and came to Nazareth."
(Luke 2:51-52).

Love, peace and joy in the presence of God. Such was the life of the Holy Family. If we wish for our homes to participate in this mystery, then we must visit the school of the Holy Family at Nazareth: "Nazareth is a kind of school where we may begin to discover what Christ's life was like and even to understand his Gospel" *(Pope St. Paul VI, January 5, 1964).*

The Holy Family at Nazareth was simultaneously a devout Jewish home and the first Christian family. The Jewish family was called to profoundly unite three critical areas of family life to God:

- The spousal relationship between husband and wife *(Cf. Exodus 20:14; Exodus 20:17; Leviticus 15:19ff).*
- The dinner table *(Cf. Kosher and Challah Laws).*
- The use of time *(Cf. Exodus 20:8 and Leviticus 23:4-43).*

Within the context of the Jewish life of the Holy Family, an angel was sent to help Mary and Joseph understand that God would profoundly dwell in their midst:

- To Mary, the angel promised that God would become Incarnate within her *(Cf. Luke 1:35).*
- To Joseph, the angel promised that God would become Incarnate in another person, i.e. Mary *(Cf. Matthew 1:20).*

Finally, the Christian family was formed when Joseph, in an act of superabundant mercy, received Mary into his home *(Cf. Matthew 1:19).*

Considering the life of the Holy Family at Nazareth, we are able to identify seven essential steps:

- Honor your wedding vows.
- Use money for other people.
- Give God some of your time.
- Set your mind on the things above.
- Find God in yourself.
- Find God in other people.
- Practice superabundant mercy.

If we learn from the Holy Family how to truly live these seven steps, then our homes will begin to experience something of the love, peace and joy of Nazareth—even in the midst of this fallen world.

Honor Your Wedding Vows

"They become one flesh." *(Genesis 2:24)*

Through the Torah, God identified the three most critical areas in the home—the spousal union, the dinner table and the use of time. The starting point is the spousal union. From it, the family and home are born.

The most fundamental understanding of the spousal union goes back to its institution in the Garden of Eden: "Therefore a man leaves his father and his mother and clings to his wife, and they become one flesh" *(Genesis 2:24)*. "One flesh" speaks to exclusivity and permanence. The union established by husband and wife is called to be mutually exclusive and to endure unto death.

This understanding should be combined with the account of creation given in the first chapter of Genesis: "And God blessed them ... 'Be fruitful and multiply, and fill the earth and subdue it; and have dominion over the fish of the sea and over the birds of the air and over every living thing that moves upon the earth" *(Genesis 1:28)*. The "one flesh" union of husband and wife is the primordial channel through which God blesses creation.

As such, it is easy to see the importance of maintaining a strong spousal union. It is also easy to see why Satan attacks the union of man and woman from the beginning: "Sin and death have entered into man's history in some way through the very heart of that unity ... formed by the man and woman" *(Pope St. John Paul II, March 5, 1980)*.

Satan continues to attack the "one flesh" union of husband and wife today Approximately, forty percent of first marriages in the United States end in divorce. The surest and fastest pathway to divorce are:

- Infidelity—more than quadruples the probability of divorce.
- Substance abuse—triples the probability of divorce.
- Money issues—more than doubles the probability of divorce.

Fortunately, there are very simple, tangible steps that can be taken to strengthen the spousal bond. It's as simple as 1-2-3-A-B-C *(See page 17)*.

Use Money for Others

"He who is kind to the poor lends to the Lord." *(Proverbs 19:17)*

The second critical area of the home identified in the Torah was the dinner table. It was essential for building community:

- Between the family members.
- Between the family and greater society through acts of charity.
- Between the family and God.

On the practical level, the Kosher laws in the Torah almost assured that Jewish families would eat together. Spending time together helped to build community within the home. Further, eating food releases dopamine and oxytocin in the brain, which helps to bind families together. This neurological reality is confirmed in numerous social studies linking together family harmony and eating family meals together.

The laws in the Torah went further. They required Jews to share a portion of their food with others *(Cf. Numbers 15:20)*. In an agrarian society, food was money. As such, the Torah required charity or generosity, which helped to build community within the larger Jewish culture. Once again, there's some important brain chemistry involved. Our brain gives us a dopamine reward every time we are charitable or help another person. We are neurologically driven to be kind to other people.

Unfortunately, things are not so simple. We are also neurologically driven to be successful, earn money and spend it on ourselves. All of these things also give us a dopamine reward. However, the brain builds a tolerance to dopamine and we must earn an ever greater salary or buy ever more amazing products to receive the same "dopamine high." Our brains literally become addicted to success.

Our current culture reinforces this more indulgent, selfish use of money. Not surprisingly, Americans are working longer and harder than ever before ...making it hard to get to the dinner table together. Further, since we can always buy more than we can afford, financial issues have typically been one of the major issues contributing to marital tension. Indeed, in the first year of marriage, financial issues are the number one strain on newlywed couples.

Fortunately, there are very simple, tangible steps so that money can be used to promote community versus foster tension. It's as simple as 1-2-3-A-B-C *(See page 17).*

Give God Some of Your Time

"Remember the Sabbath day, to keep it holy." *(Exodus 20:8)*

The third critical area in the home identified in the Torah was the use of time. Time is a gift from God. Each time we receive a gift from God, we are called to give or tithe a portion back to him. The Torah commanded Israel to give a portion of each unit of time back to God:

- **The Day:** Israel was to offer a morning and evening sacrifice *(Cf. Exodus 29:38-39).*

- **The Week:** Israel was to keep holy the Sabbath *(Cf. Exodus 20:8).*

- **The Month:** Israel was to celebrate the feast of the new moon *(Cf. Numbers 28:11).*

- **The Year:** The Torah established an entire liturgical calendar to be followed throughout the year *(Cf. Leviticus 23:1-36).*

- **The Lifetime:** During the normal course of events, every Jew would experience a Jubilee once in his or her lifetime *(Cf. Leviticus 25:10).*

Now here's the amazing part. When we give time to God, he uses it to transform us so that we receive the benefits. Neurologically speaking, prayer increases activity in the anterior cingulate cortex making us more empathetic and compassionate. It decreases activity in the amygdala reducing fear and anxiety. Practically speaking, it reduces substance abuse, irritating habits, materialism and infidelity. Put it all together and it is easy to see that giving time to God (prayer) increases marital and family satisfaction and decreases the probability of divorce.

Unfortunately, the average American only spends 8.4 minutes in prayer each day! Of course, there are many different reasons people don't take time to pray. But, in reality, most people simply let themselves be "distracted" by a host of other options—some of which are necessary, some of which are not. The average American spends almost three hours on the media each day. We will never run out of alternatives to prayer. As such, we must consciously choose to pray.

Fortunately, there are very simple, tangible steps you can take to help you give time to God so that God can give a more superabundant life to you. It's as simple as 1-2-3-A-B-C *(See page 17).*

Set Your Mind on the Things Above

"Be transformed by the renewal of your mind." *(Romans 12:2)*

Into the very Jewish life of the Holy Family, God sent an angel with a message. Ultimately, it was a message about God's presence in their life: "I dwell in the high and holy place, and also with him who is of a contrite and humble spirit" *(Isaiah 57:15)*. God would be present in the Holy Family in a unique and unrepeatable way. They would live a life "hidden with Christ in God" *(Colossians 3:3)*.

The key word is "hidden." The life of the Holy Family at Nazareth forms part of Christ's hidden life. Their life was so ordinary that their neighbors were scandalized when Christ began his public ministry: "Coming to his own country Jesus taught them in their synagogue, so that they were astonished, and said, 'Where did this man get his wisdom … Is this not the carpenter's son?' … And they took offense at him" *(Matthew 13:54-57)*.

The challenge for Mary and St. Joseph was to find Christ in the midst of their normal, everyday, family life. To do so, they had to ponder the ways of God: "Mary kept all these things, pondering them in her heart" *(Luke 2:19)*. By "setting their minds on the things above" *(Colossians 3:2)*, they were able to find the Scriptures being fulfilled in their own lives.

We must also ponder God's presence in our midst. The perfect aid is Scripture: "Your word is a lamp to my feet and a light to my path" *(Psalm 119:105)*. We should read the Bible frequently enough that scriptural verses spontaneously come to our mind throughout the course of our everyday lives. When they do so, we will be able to keep our minds set on Christ.

To keep your mind fixed on Christ is a true mental and interior discipline. We are engulfed by distractions and an endless barrage of images and messages. We must turn to Our Lady and St. Joseph to help us live an interior life … where we will find God.

Find God in Yourself

"The [Holy] Spirit ... dwells with you, and will be in you." *(John 14:17)*

The message of the angel about God's presence in the home was very personal. God would dwell within the family members. To Mary, the angel said, "The Holy Spirit will come upon you, and the power of the Most High will overshadow you, therefore the child to be born will be called holy, the Son of God" *(Luke 1:35)*. Mary was to find God dwelling within herself.

We have likewise received a promise of God's presence within us: "If a man loves me, he will keep my word ... and we will come to him and make our home with him" *(John 14:23)*. Further, we have been promised that this indwelling will be very personal: "He who eats my flesh and drinks my blood abides in me, and I in him" *(John 6:56)*. Through the Eucharist, Jesus Christ—Body, Blood, Soul and Divinity—dwells within us.

In a certain sense, the Eucharist perpetuates the mystery of the Incarnation: "Though it is a unique and unrepeatable event, the Incarnation of the Word in the Blessed Virgin Mary's womb is sacramentally perpetuated in the Eucharistic celebration, which makes God present with us" *(Jesus Living in Mary: Handbook of the Spirituality of St. Louis Marie de Montfort, 1994, p. 386)*. The awe inspiring reality is that, in a certain sense, the Eucharist perpetuates the mystery of the Incarnation in us.

To find God dwelling within, we must become ever more focused upon the Eucharist. When we receive the Eucharist, we must encounter Christ in silence: "For God alone my soul waits in silence" *(Psalm 62:1)*. We must extend this moment throughout the day by frequently taking a moment to silence external distractions and turn inward to speak with God dwelling within.

The ability to find God dwelling within is—like all things in the spiritual life—a combination of God's grace and human effort. This was the life of Charles de Foucauld. The grace of a radical conversion. The human effort to build a little Nazareth where he could abide in God's presence. Let us pray for the grace to form our homes into a little Nazareth.

Find God Dwelling in Other People

"The Son of God has united Himself in some fashion with every man."
(Gaudium et Spes, #22)

The angel's message about God's presence in the home at Nazareth went further. The angel told St. Joseph: "Joseph, son of David, do not fear to take Mary your wife, for that which is conceived in her is of the Holy Spirit" *(Matthew 1:20)*. St. Joseph was to find God dwelling in another person, Mary.

We have also received promises that we can find God in our family members:

- **The spousal union:** "For where two or three are gathered in my name, there am I in the midst of them" *(Matthew 18:20)*. We seal our marriages in the name of the Blessed Trinity. "Shelly, receive this ring as a sign of my love and fidelity. In the name of the Father, and of the Son, and of the Holy Spirit. Amen." Since we seal our marriages in the name of the Blessed Trinity, God is dwelling in them by definition. Marriage is a "great sacrament" *(Cf. Ephesians 5:32)*.

- **The parent-child relationship:** "Whoever receives one such child in my name receives me" *(Matthew 18:5)*. Christ is walking up to us in our children.

Our Lady helped Don Bosco to radically live this reality. She helped Don Bosco find Christ in the homeless boys of Turin: "As you did it to one of the least of these my brethren, you did it to me" *(Matthew 25:40)*. Knowing that he was serving Christ, Don Bosco served the boys with great joy. Indeed, he founded a festive oratory so that the boys could "have full liberty to jump, run and make as much noise as they please." Those festive oratories radiated the joy of Nazareth.

Christ also wishes our families to experience the joy of Nazareth: "That my joy may be in you, and that your joy may be full" *(John 15:11)*. Imagine the impact on your home if every day you consciously sought to bring joy to your family members. Imagine the impact on your own spiritual life. We should pray for the grace to find God dwelling in our family members ... and then to bring them the joy of Nazareth.

Practice Superabundant Mercy

"The Gentiles might glorify God for his mercy." *(Romans 15:9)*

Jesus Christ came to reveal the mystery of the Father: "He who has seen me has seen the Father" *(John 14:9)*. Since the Word abides "in the bosom of the Father" *(John 1:18)*, it is a revelation that only he can make. Ultimately, Jesus reveals that the heart of the Father is "rich in mercy" *(Ephesians 2:4)*.

Christ makes the revelation of the Father's mercy not so much by words, but in actions: "God sent the Son into the world, not to condemn the world, but that the world might be saved through him" *(John 3:19)*. The entire life and public ministry of Christ is a revelation of the Father's mercy. Nonetheless, this revelation reaches its climax with Christ's sacrifice upon the Cross: "Greater love has no man than this, that a man lay down his life for his friends. You are my friends" *(John 15:13)*.

Ultimately, the sacrifice of Christ had a familial dimension. Christ offered himself for his Bride, the Church: "Husbands, love your wives, as Christ loved the Church and gave himself up for her ... that he might present the Church to himself in splendor, without spot or wrinkle or any such thing" *(Ephesians 5:25-27)*. It is the loving sacrifice of the bridegroom that purifies the bride. Christ has asked us to follow his example: "I have given you an example, that you also should do" *(John 13:15)*. We are called to become rich in mercy: "Be merciful, even as your Father is merciful" *(Luke 6:36)*.

St. Therese pierced the mystery of the power of loving sacrifice. She offered herself as an oblation to the merciful love of God. To remain faithful to this gift, she offered every single action of every single moment of every single day as a gift of love to God. This is the dynamism of the "little way." It is a love so overwhelming that it must be expressed always and everywhere ... in the most hidden manner ... as so many hidden glances between the lover and the beloved.

Such is our calling. Such is the true lesson of the School of Nazareth.

Living the Seven Steps:
It's as Simple as 1-2-3-A-B-C

The Seven Steps truly have the ability to help your family share in the love, peace and joy of the Holy Family at Nazareth. Getting started is simple ... it's just not easy. Here are three simple actions for each of the first three steps that can make a profound difference in the life of your family.

STEP 1: HONOR YOUR WEDDING VOWS

- **Substantially reduce the media:** Neurologically, the brain processes images as if they were real. Pornography and other sexual images are a type of "virtual infidelity." Consumption of highly sexualized media is correlated with reduced marital satisfaction.
- **Go to bed together:** It helps align schedules and leads to greater marital satisfaction.
- **End the day with 15 minutes together with your spouse:** Developing and maintaining friendships is dependent upon time spent in shared activities. This is also true for the spousal union.

STEP 2: USE MONEY FOR OTHERS

- **Substantially reduce the media:** Studies indicate that media consumption leads to increased materialism and increased tension within the family.
- **Eat dinner together at least 5 nights per week:** Along with going to bed together, this helps to align schedules leading to greater family cohesion. Studies indicate eating together on a regular basis leads to better relationships within the family.
- **Tithe to the Church:** Studies reveal that we receive greater satisfaction from giving money away than we do from spending money on ourselves. Begin by giving money to God.

STEP 3: GIVE GOD SOME OF YOUR TIME

- **Substantially reduce the media:** Average Americans spend 8.4 minutes in prayer per day and almost 3 hours per day on the media. The simplest way to "find time" to pray is to reallocate time from the media.
- **Pray the Rosary every day:** The Rosary is the prayer most recommended by the Church. Neurological studies reveal it to be one of the most transformative prayers.
- **Begin and end each day with at least 10 minutes of prayer:** Prayer literally changes structures within the brain reducing fear and making you more compassionate. However, it takes time to receive the benefits. The more the better.

The Spiritual Journey

"So faith, hope and love abide, these three; but the greatest of these is love." *(1 Corinthians 13:13)*

The life of the Holy Family at Nazareth was a type of Paradise on earth Unfortunately, we are no longer in Paradise. After the Original Sin of Adam and Eve, humanity was expelled from Paradise and we have been struggling to return ever since. Fortunately, the Church has contemplated this mystery for the past two thousand years and has helped identify the path that leads back to an encounter with God.

Almost 1500 years ago, Pseudo-Dionysius identified three stages through which God leads the soul to prepare it for union with him: "What we humans call the beatitude of God is … purifying, illuminating, and perfecting" *(Pseudo-Dionysius, Celestial Hierarchy, 3.2)*. As such, the three stages have typically been identified as:

- **The Purgative Stage** or the "Way of Beginners" where the soul is purged of its disordered passions and desires that lead to selfishness and isolation.
- **The Illuminative Stage** or the "Way of Proficients" where the mind is illumined to spiritual realities and the path leading to God.
- **The Unitive Stage** or the "Way of the Perfect" where the soul attains to union with God and experiences a joy and peace that are "not of this world."

The journey through these three stages has historically been shrouded in mystery and reserved for the "few" who find the "narrow gate" *(Cf. Matthew 7:13-14)*. Almost 500 years ago, St. John of the Cross and St. Theresa of Avila traveled this narrow path and left mystical writings that soar to an encounter with God.

Each of our four saints drank deeply of these writings and … were granted access to the school at Nazareth. Guided by Our Lady, they left for us a path perfectly suited to lay men and women living in the family. Indeed, their path helps us to fulfill the words of Pope Francis: "Those who have deep spiritual aspirations [should] see [the family] as a path which the Lord is using to lead them to the heights of mystical union" *(Pope Francis, Amoris Laetitia, #316)*. The narrow path to God remains difficult, but it passes right by your front door.

The Purgative Stage

"He must increase, but I must decrease." *(John 3:30)*

The spiritual journey begins when God enkindles love in the heart: "Fired with love's urgent longings" *(St. John of the Cross, Dark Night, Stanza 1)*. The soul feels a great desire for God ... but quickly discovers there are challenges. As a result of Original Sin, the human person has become interiorly disordered: "The harmony in which they had found themselves ... is now destroyed: the control of the soul's spiritual faculties over the body is shattered" *(Catechism, #400)*. As such, everyone on the spiritual journey must enter into a purgative stage.

This interior disorder impacts three critical areas: "For all that is in the world, the concupiscence of the flesh and the concupiscence of the eyes and the pride of life" *(1 John 2:16)*. Thus, the flesh, the world and the devil (who tempts us to pride) are the three enemies in the spiritual life. Further, to a certain extent, the disorder in these three areas has been internalized or "written into the body" *(Cf. Romans 7:15-23)*.

For example, we are driven by the brain's reward system to earn money and to use that money to provide for our families and those in need. This would be the proper use of money. However, the brain's reward system also drives us to earn money for its own sake and then spend it on ourselves to purchase items, frequently for the sake of indulgence or vanity.

From this example, it is easy to see that the interior disorder has caused the human person to have a tendency to selfishness. Originally, we were called to be selfless or self-giving, which is love. To find union with God, "who is love" *(1 John 4:16)*, we must be freed of our selfishness so that we are opened to self-giving. This is the goal of the purgative stage. It is also the goal of marriage and family life. Bridegroom and bride enter into a relationship of love. They are asked if they are willing to give themselves to each other in marriage. Fidelity to these vows is a sure way to be purged of selfishness and opened to love.

The Illuminative Stage

"The light shines in the darkness, and the darkness did not comprehend it" *(John 1:5)*

Having passed through the purgative stage, the soul is freed from the selfishness that prevented it from perceiving the ways of God. It now enters into a new state—the illumination stage of the spiritual life: "When I was a child, I spoke like a child, I thought like a child, I reasoned like a child; when I became a man, I gave up childish ways. For now we see in a mirror dimly, but then face to face. Now I know in part: then I shall understand fully" *(1 Corinthians 13:11-12)*.

The darkness and dryness of the purgative stage give way to a certain sweetness in the spiritual life. The soul begins to see things from a new perspective—from God's perspective. The soul also begins to experience moments of union with God. According to St. John of the Cross: "In this new state, as one liberated from a cramped prison cell, it goes about the things of God with much more freedom and satisfaction of spirit and with more abundant interior delight ... The soul readily finds ... a very serene, loving contemplation and spiritual delight" *(Dark Night, II.1.1.)*.

St. John of the Cross refers to the illuminative stage as the state of spiritual betrothal. Here the soul finds loving union with God, but not on a permanent basis. It is like lovers who are preparing for their wedding. They have tremendous joy as they long for the moment of consummation ... but still must experience periods of separation. As such, the soul also experiences moments of separation from God, which causes it great pain.

The term spiritual betrothal is an apt description since souls can readily live this stage within marriage and family life. There attentive souls will frequently catch glimpses of God's presence ... but not uninterruptedly. There will still be period of trial, separation and pain. Nonetheless, if the soul perseveres, it will be able to discern God's presence ... especially during moments of the Cross. It will then be ready to enter into the unitive stage.

The Unitive Stage

"If a man loves me ... we will come to him and make our home with him." *(John 14:23)*

Every soul is called to enter into and complete the purgative stage. Every soul is called to enter into the illuminative stage. Only a limited number of souls are invited into the unitive stage ... in this life. These are souls who have been purged of all selfishness and continually embrace the path of love. As such, these souls no longer commit sin. They still commit faults, frequently with reduced to little culpability.

The heights of this state are truly a participation in the joys of heaven ... as much as is possible in this fallen world: "The ninth step of love causes the soul to burn gently ... The Holy Spirit produces this gentle and delightful ardor by reason of the perfect soul's union with God. We cannot speak of the goods and riches of God a person enjoys on this step because even were we to write many books about them the greater part would remain unsaid" *(St. John of the Cross, Dark Night, II.20.4)*.

Joys of heaven ... in this fallen world. Suddenly, this sounds like the Holy Family at Nazareth: It "was a heaven, a paradise on earth, endless delights in this place of grief: it was a glory already begun in the vileness, abjection and lowliness of their life" *(Monsignor Jean Jacques Olier, 1608-1658)*. Souls who attain to this state pass directly into heaven without the need for purgatory. Our Lady has been assumed body and soul into heaven.

If we are willing to attend the school at Nazareth, marriage does indeed become "a path which the Lord is using to lead [us] to the heights of mystical union" *(Pope Francis, Amoris Laetitia, #316)*. Although we cannot aspire to the unitive stage under our own power, we can trust in the goodness and mercy of God. I cannot believe that our loving Father would refuse anyone who was willing to take the next step. Let us pray for an unwavering trust in the goodness of God and for the grace to be faithful to the demands of love ... until we find enduring union with God.

Discerning the Spiritual Journey

The soul's state along the spiritual journey is, properly speaking, discerned by a spiritual director/mentor who has the appropriate training and personal spiritual life. Among other things, this discernment involves the interplay of three critical areas:

- The objective state of sin and sinful actions in the life of the soul.
- The soul's union with God and prayer life.
- The spirit that animates the soul and its communion with God.

Notwithstanding the foregoing, we have found the following questions useful in helping the soul and/or spiritual guides in their discernment of the beginning stages of the spiritual journey. Note: This is not an examination of conscience properly speaking and not all of these items relate to sin. Further, they have been specifically adapted to those seeking to find God within the context of marriage and family life.

- **How many times per week do you go to Mass?** (0;1;2;3;4;5;6;7)

- **How many times per week do you begin your day with prayer?** *(0;1;2;3;4;5;6;7)*

- **How many times per week do you have prayer in the evening or before going to bed?** *(0;1;2;3;4;5;6;7)*

- **How much time do you spend in prayer each day (excluding Mass)?** *(none; less than 15 min; less than 30 min; less than one hour; more than one hour)*

- **How frequently do you go to Confession?** *(once/week; more than monthly; once/month; several per year; a few times a year; 1-2 per year; less than once/year)*

- **How frequently do you read Scripture?** *(Daily; more than once/week; weekly; more than monthly; monthly; several per year; less than once per year; never)*

- **How frequently do you say the Rosary?** *(Daily; more than once/week; weekly; more than monthly; monthly; several per year; less than once per year; never)*

- **How many nights per week do you go to bed together with your spouse (defined as being in bed together before either person is asleep)?** *(0;1;2;3;4;5;6;7)*

- **When was the last time you raised your voice in anger with your spouse?** *(this week; this month; this year; over 1 year; over 5 years)*

Discerning the Spiritual Journey

- When was the last time you withheld affection from your spouse? *(this week; this month; this year; over 1 year; over 5 years)*

- When was the last time you flirted with or received the attention of some one other than your spouse? *(this week; this month; this year; over 1 year; over 5 years)*

- What type of contraception do you use? For postmenopausal couples, What type of contraception did you use? *(Trying to get pregnant; none; NFP; condom; the Pill; vasectomy/tubal ligation; other)*

- What percentage of your before tax income do you give to charity including the Church? *(none; 1-2; 3-4; 5-6; 7-8; 9-10; over 10)*

- How many nights per week do you do work from home (before the children are in bed)? *(0;1;2;3;4;5;6;7)*

- When was the last time you had an argument with your spouse or child about money or purchasing something? *(this week; this month; this year; more than 1 year; more than 5 years)*

- How many nights per week do you eat dinner with the family members that are living at home? *(0;1;2;3;4;5;6;7)*

- How many nights per week is some type of media on during dinner or technology brought to the dinner table? *(0;1;2;3;4;5;6;7)*

- How much time you spend on the media each day (television, computer not work related, social media, music, video games, etc.)? *(none; less than 15 minutes; less than 30 minutes; less than one hour; less than 2 hours; less than 3 hours; more than 3 hours)*

- How many movies do you watch per week? *(None; 1;2;3;4;5;more than 5)*

- When was the last time you watched an R-rated movie containing nudity or graphic violence? *(this week, this month, this year, over 1 year; over 5 years)*

- When was the last time you intentionally viewed pornography? (this week; this month; this year; over 1 year; over 5 years)

- Do you agree with all of the Church's teachings? *(yes / no)* If not, which ones do you disagree with?

The Challenges and Support in the Spiritual Life

As we journey to God through the three stages of the spiritual life, we will encounter three critical obstacles, which Christ identifies for us in the parable of the Sower and the Seed:

"A sower went out to sow ... Some seeds fell along the path and the birds came and devoured them ... [this is those who] hear the word of the kingdom ... [but] the Evil One comes and snatches away what is sown in his heart ... Other seeds fell on rocky ground ... immediately they sprang up ... but when the sun rose they were scorched ... [this is those who] has no root in himself, but endures for a while ... [but] when tribulation or persecution arise on account of the word, immediately he falls away ... Other seeds fell upon thorns ... This is he who hears the word, but the cares of the world and the delight in riches choke the word, and it proves unfruitful" *(Matthew 13:3-23)*.

In this parable, Christ identifies the three enemies or challenges in the spiritual life: the flesh, the world and the devil. Unfortunately, because of Original Sin, a "disorder" has been written into our bodies in each of these three areas: "I do not do what I want, but I do the very thing I hate" *(Romans 7:15)*. As such, we will confront these three challenges our entire life.

The spiritual journey is a long and arduous path. Fortunately, Christ has provided us with three spiritual foods to sustain us on this journey:

- **The Word of God:** "Man shall not live by bread alone, but by every word that proceeds from the mouth of God" *(Matthew 4:4)*.
- **The Will of God:** "My food is to do the will of him who sent me" *(John 4:33)*.
- **The Eucharist:** "My flesh is food indeed, and my blood is drink indeed" *(John 6:55)*.

We must learn to bring these three spiritual foods into our homes so that our entire family may journey to God. Don Bosco, St. Therese and St. Charles de Foucauld will be the perfect guides to help us do so.

The Challenge of the Flesh

The first challenge in the spiritual life is "weaknesses of the flesh," which includes all 7 of the deadly or capital sins – pride, lust, greed, envy, anger, sloth and gluttony. Nonetheless, in our current culture, people most frequently associate "sins of the flesh" with sexual sin.

The union of man and woman was God's crowning gift to humanity in our innocence: "Therefore a man leaves his father and his mother and clings to his wife, and they become one flesh. And the man and his wife were both naked, and were not ashamed" *(Genesis 2:24-25)*.

The human brain has three systems critically important in facilitating the union between man and woman:

- **The Attraction System,** which is part of the brain's reward system and activates in less than one second when a man or woman identify a prospective mate.
- **The Romantic Love System,** which is also part of the brain's reward system. It activates over time and helps an individual re-prioritize his/her life to do all the things necessary to form a unique bond with the beloved.
- **The Attachment System,** which involves the trust and self-awareness centers in the brain. This is the slowest of the three systems. It takes time to build trust … and to restructure the brain so profoundly that a "pair bond" is established between the lover and the beloved. It is the neurological realization of "one flesh."

After the Fall, these three systems do not always work in harmony. The attraction system may activate, but then turn towards objectification versus romantic love. The attachment system may have formed a pair bond (i.e. marriage), but then the attraction system identifies an alternative.

Living our 7 Steps, 1-2-3-A-B-C, will help us to reorder these systems correctly:

- **Minimize the media,** it only activates the attraction system, followed by objectification.
- **Go to bed together,** physical touch is important for both activating and maintaining the Romantic Love and Attachment systems.
- **Spend 15 minutes per day talking with your spouse,** when this includes remembering and celebrating the relationship it reactivates the same neuro circuits as the original experience—strengthening the Romantic Love and Attachment systems.

The Challenge of the World

The second challenge in the spiritual life is "the world." This includes the desire to be successful, important in the eyes of the world, popular or well known, etc. In our culture, this frequently relates to our career and could be anything from being a sports celebrity, to the media, to the financial markets, to technology …

The ability and desire to work was a great gift from God to humanity in its innocence: "The Lord God took the man and put him in the garden of Eden to till it and keep it" *(Genesis 2:15)*. This helped to reveal man's dignity. Created to the "image and likeness" *(Genesis 1:26)* of God, man was called to become a "co-creator" by cooperating with God in the work of creation.

Many brain structures are involved in our orientation towards the world and a full discussion is well beyond the scope of these few words. However, the following should be noted:

- **Creativity:** Several networks are involved in creativity including the default, salience and executive networks. Significantly, we receive a dumping of dopamine from the brain's reward system when we have a "creative moment." We are driven to become creative.
- **Success:** Creativity frequently leads to success, including monetary success. The brain's reward system drives us to be successful and earn a living.
- **Generosity:** The brain's reward system drives us to use our resources to be generous with others.

However, since the Fall, our orientation towards the world is disordered:

- **Dopamine tolerance:** The brain builds a tolerance to dopamine, requiring ever greater amounts to "feel the buzz," which can lead to an addiction to success.
- **Selfishness:** The brain's reward system also provides a dumping of dopamine when we purchase goods for ourselves, which can lead to selfishness.

Living our 7 Steps, 1-2-3-A-B-C, will help us to reorder these systems correctly:

- **Minimize the media,** it places material goods in the brain as an object to be sought to bring happiness.
- **Eat dinner together 5 nights per week,** it helps us to reorder money to its first goal, to provide for our family.
- **Give money to charity,** which helps us to activate the brain's generosity system.

The Challenge of the Devil and Pride

The final and ultimate challenge in the spiritual life is the devil. He tempted Adam and Eve in the Garden of Eden. He tempted Christ at the beginning of Christ's public ministry. He tempts men and women of today—including me and you. Ultimately, Satan attempts to include us in his own pride and rebellion against God:

"How you are fallen from heaven … You said in your heart, '… I will ascend above the heights of the clouds, I will make myself like the Most High.' But you are brought down to Sheol, to the depths of the Pit" *(Isaiah 14:12-15)*.

To trap us in his rebellion, Satan must separate us from God. We were created to be sons and daughters of God and to abide in his presence. The desire for God has been written in our bodies:

- **Prayer:** the brain's reward system gives us a dumping of dopamine whenever we pray. We are driven to pray.

Nonetheless, since Original Sin in the Garden of Eden, humanity has been hiding from God. Our relationship with God has become disordered:

- **Pride:** An area of the medial prefrontal cortex causes us to perceive ourselves as better than we actually are—smarter, funnier, more attractive, etc.

Humility is the ability to see ourselves as we really are. Ultimately, it is to see ourselves as God sees us—to see ourselves through his eyes. Living our 7 Steps, 1-2-3-A-B-C, will help us to reorder these systems correctly:

- **Minimize the media:** Currently, the average American spends almost 3 hours per day on the media and only 8.4 minutes per day on his/her prayer life. Let us begin by reallocating time from the media to God.
- **Pray the Rosary every day:** The Rosary helps us to contemplate the mysteries of Jesus' life. It helps us to pattern our life on Jesus' life.
- **Begin and end each day with 10 minutes of silence:** Frequently, most of our prayer time is spent in us talking to God. We need to include moments of silence so that God can speak to us. When we listen to God, we will begin to see ourselves in the way he sees us.

The Word of God

To sustain us on the long, arduous journey through the three stages of the spiritual life, God has provided us with three spiritual foods. The first one identified in Scripture is the Word of God. It was revealed during Christ's temptation in the desert: "The tempter came and said to [Jesus], 'If you are the Son of God, command these stones to become loaves of bread.' But he answered, 'It is written, Man shall not live by bread alone, but by every word that proceeds from the mouth of God'" *(Matthew 4:3-4)*.

The Word of God is specifically food for our intellect. It helps us to understand the path God has laid out for us: "Your word is a lamp to my feet and a light to my path" *(Psalm 119:105)*. It especially helps us to discover God's presence in our lives: You search the scriptures, because you think that in them you have eternal life; and it is they that bear witness to me" *(John 5:39)*.

This was the mystery that St. Therese lived. She went through a period of deep doubt in her spiritual life where she questioned the path she had taken. Finally, through the Scriptures, God brought Therese great clarity: "During my meditation, my desires caused me a veritable martyrdom, and I opened the Epistles of St. Paul to find some kind of answer ... and the Apostle explain[ed] how all the most perfect gifts are nothing without love ... I understood that Love comprised all vocations ... that it embraced all times and places ... that it was eternal. Then in the excess of my delirious joy, I cried out: O Jesus, my Love ... my vocation, at last I have found it ... my vocation is Love."

God also wishes to speak to you through the Scriptures. The time honored method for allowing God to speak through the Scriptures is called *Lectio Divina*. When we read Scripture slowly, pondering its meaning in our heart, God is able to help us see how it applies to our life personally. Further, when we practice *Lectio Divina* together with our family members, God is present in our midst opening the Scriptures. *(Turn to p. 38 to learn more about Lectio Divina.)*

The Will of God

The second spiritual food was revealed to us in Christ's encounter with the Samaritan woman at the well near the start of his public ministry. "Jesus, wearied as he was with his journey, sat down beside the well ... There came a woman of Samaria to draw water. Jesus said to her, 'Give me a drink' ... the disciples begged him, saying, 'Rabbi, eat.' But he said to them, 'I have food to eat of which you do not know ... my food is to do the will of him who sent me, and to accomplish his work'" *(John 4:6-34)*.

We are called to feed on the will of God. Fortunately, Scripture lets us know God's will for each and every person: "This is the will of God, your sanctification" *(1 Thessalonians 4:3)*. We are called to become holy. In Judaism, to be holy was to be set aside and consecrated to God. To be "set aside" means that we must be different. Our lives cannot be enslaved to the three challenges in the spiritual life. Instead, they must be given to God.

Don Bosco understood this calling. He cultivated in his festive oratory a climate of sanctity: "He imbues his boys with such a spirit of piety that he almost inebriates them. The very atmosphere which surrounds them, the air they breathe is impregnated with religion ... [the boys] would have to move directly against the current to become bad ... Sanctity was in the air you breathed. You did not notice its presence so much as its absence the moment you left" *(Give Me Souls, pp. 149-151)*. If we learn from Don Bosco how to model our homes after his festive oratory, then they will begin to resemble the holiness of the home of the Holy Family at Nazareth.

Nonetheless, each of us must adapt the festive oratory to our personal and family lives. The next section helps us to develop a spiritual plan of life perfectly suited to our personal spiritual journey and circumstances.

The Eucharist

During his discourse on the bread of life, Christ revealed the Eucharist—his own flesh and blood—to be our ultimate spiritual food and drink: "I am the living bread which came down from heaven; if any one eats of this bread, he will live for ever ... For my flesh is food indeed, and my blood is drink indeed. He who eats my flesh and drinks my blood abides in me, and I in him" *(John 6:51-56)*. The Eucharist is the bread from heaven given for our spiritual journey. It is an invaluable aid in the "Practice of the Presence of God" where we simply abide in God's presence within our souls.

Such was the life of St. Charles de Foucauld. When he sought to form his monastery into a "little Nazareth," he became ever more Eucharistic. "You are there, my Lord Jesus, in the Holy Eucharist. You are there but a few feet from me in the tabernacle. Your body, your soul, your humanity, your divinity, your entire being is there in its double nature! How close you are, God!" *(Charles de Foucauld, p.154)*. Like St. Charles, we must become ever more Eucharistic.

But we must go further. Our family members and our marriages are a type of "living tabernacle" where Christ is present. When our family members received Christ in the Eucharist, he continues to reside in them: "We will come to him and make our home with him" *(John 14:23)*. Further, Christ is present in the midst of our marital union: "Where two or three are gathered in my name, there am I in the midst of them" *(Matthew 18:20)*. There is a profound bond between the Eucharist and the marital union: "The Eucharist is the very source of Christian marriage ... In [it], Christian spouses encounter the source from which their own marriage covenant flows, is interiorly structured and continuously renewed" *(Pope John Paul II, Familiaris Consortio, #57)*.

If we are to successfully navigate our spiritual journey, then we must feed on Christ himself—substantially in the Eucharist where he is present Body, Blood, Soul and Divinity, but also in our family members.

Building a
Spiritual Plan of Life

One of Shelly's favorite sayings is, "A 'what' without a 'when' is a 'never.'" She's right. If you truly desire to make progress in your spiritual life and share in the love, peace, and joy of the Holy Family at Nazareth, then you must systematically apply the 7 Steps to your life. You must set aside time to transition your holy desires into actionable steps that transform you and your family. This plan must be robust and tangible. Further, after surveying thousands of people across the country, I can tell you that the #1 determinate of progress in the spiritual life is the relative balance between the time spent on the media versus time spent on the spiritual life.

Scripture encourages us to pray seven times a day: "Seven times a day I praise you" *(Psalm 119:146)*. Priests and religious fulfill this by praying the Divine Office or Liturgy of the Hours. The Divine Office is based upon the Psalms, which are said at seven different times each day. Over the course of four weeks, the entire 150 psalms are recited ... along with other prayers. This is a wonderful prayer and I try to say a portion of it each day. Nonetheless, it is not well suited for that average lay person living in the world with a family. The monthly magazine, *The Magnificat*, has a simplified version for the laity that I highly recommend. Nonetheless, many lay people still find this challenging.

As such, I've tried to adapt the principles of the Divine Office with the 7 Steps of Nazareth into seven actions that can be the foundation of a systematic and robust spiritual life:

- Morning Prayer
- Midday Prayer
- Night Prayer
- The Most Holy Rosary
- Reading of Scripture using *Lectio Divina*
- Liturgy of the Dinner Table
- Practice of the Presence of God

We will begin by discussing the "what" we want to do, then we will identify the "when" we will do them. Although these steps have been developed for the average lay person living and working in the world, they will take effort. They are simple, but not easy. Further, the spirit with which they are lived is the true sign of spiritual progress.

Morning Prayer

The "hinges" of the Divine Office are morning and evening prayer. You should begin and end your day in prayer. Your morning prayer should be long enough to center you in God so profoundly that you remain in him throughout the day. I recommend four specific actions for morning prayer:

(1) Consecration of the day to Our Lady;
(2) Protection Prayer;
(3) Canticle of Zechariah (Benedictus); and
(4) Paradisus Dei's Prayer for the New Evangelization.

1. CONSECRATION TO OUR LADY

Dear Mother, I consecrate myself and this day to you, in the mystery of your Immaculate Conception, totus tuus. Ease the doubts, the fears and the distractions of my mind. Give me to drink of your desire; and let your fiat be resplendent in my life. Amen.

2. PROTECTION PRAYERS
(CHOOSE WHICHEVER SPEAK TO YOU.)

Angel of God

Angel of God, my guardian dear,
to whom God's love commits you here.
Ever this day (or night) be at my side
to light, to guard, to rule and guide.
Amen.

Prayer for the Protection of St. Joseph

To you, O blessed Joseph,
do we come in our tribulation,
and having implored the help of your most holy Spouse,
we confidently invoke your patronage also.

Through that charity which bound you
to the Immaculate Virgin Mother of God
and through the paternal love
with which you embraced the Child Jesus,
we humbly beg you graciously to regard the inheritance
which Jesus Christ has purchased by his Blood,
and with your power and strength to aid us in our necessities.

O most watchful guardian of the Holy Family,
defend the chosen children of Jesus Christ;
O most loving father, ward off from us
every contagion of error and corrupting influence;
O our most mighty protector, be kind to us
and from heaven assist us in our struggle
with the power of darkness.

As once you rescued the Child Jesus from deadly peril,
so now protect God's Holy Church
from the snares of the enemy and from all adversity;
shield, too, each one of us by your constant protection,
so that, supported by your example and your aid,
we may be able to live piously, to die in holiness,
and to obtain eternal happiness in heaven.
Amen.

Prayer to St. Michael the Archangel

St. Michael the Archangel, defend us in battle.
Be our protection against the wickedness and snares of the Devil.
My God rebuke him, we humbly pray;
and do thou, O Prince of the heavenly hosts,
by the power of God,
cast into hell Satan, and all the evil spirits
who prowl throughout the world seeking the ruin of souls.
Amen.

3. CANTICLE OF ZECHARIAH (BENEDICTUS):
— *Recited in the Divine Office in Morning Prayer (Luke 1:68-79)*

Blessed be the Lord, the God of Israel:
he has come to his people and set them free.
He has raised up for us a mighty savior,
born of the house of his servant David.
Through his holy prophets he promised of old
that he would save us from our enemies,
from the hands of all who hate us.
He promised to show mercy to our fathers
and to remember his holy covenant.
This was the oath he swore to our father Abraham:
to set us free from the hands of our enemies,
free to worship him without fear,
holy and righteous in his sight all the days of our life.

You my child, shall be called the prophet of the Most High;
for you will go before the Lord to prepare his way,
to give his people knowledge of salvation
by the forgiveness of their sins.
In the tender compassion of our God
the dawn from on high shall break upon us,
to shine on those who dwell in darkness and the shadow of death,
and to guide our feet into the way of peace.

Glory be to the Father, and to the Son and to the Holy Spirit.
As it was in the beginning, is now and ever shall be
world without end.
Amen.

4. PARADISUS DEI PRAYER FOR THE NEW EVANGELIZATION

Heavenly Mother, spotless bride of the spotless Lamb,
your children stand gathered together before you.
With St. Joseph and the apostle John, we wish to bring you into our home,
so that you may open to us the treasures of your Immaculate Heart.
Reveal to us the hidden face of your Son, present in our midst.
Teach us to trust in the abundance of the Father's mercy.
Make us docile to the voice of the Spirit echoing in our depths.
Grant that the seeds of grace sown in us would not be lost,
but blossom forth unto life everlasting.

Dawn of Salvation, Star of the New Evangelization,
grant that the darkness may not prevail over the light.
Together with Saint John Paul II, we consecrate ourselves to you in
the mystery of your Immaculate Conception, Totus Tuus.
Send us into the great mission field of the family,
so that among all the nations, the praise of God may resound on the
lips of infants and of babes.
By the grace of God, in the power of the Holy Spirit,
help us to build a civilization worthy of the human person,
created male and female, created in the image and likeness of the
Triune God, who is love.
Amen.

Midday Prayer

The Angelus

— Said at all times other than during the Easter Season

The Angel of the Lord declared unto Mary.
And she conceived by the Holy Spirit.
(Hail Mary, full of grace, the Lord is with thee. Blessed art thou among
women and blessed is the fruit of thy womb, Jesus. Holy Mary, Mother of
God, pray for us sinners, now and at the hour of our death. Amen.)

Behold the handmaid of the Lord.
Be it done unto me according to thy word.
(Hail Mary)

And the Word was made flesh.
And dwelt among us.
(Hail Mary)

Prayer for us, O Holy Mother of God;
that we may be made worthy of the promises of Christ.

Let us pray:
Pour forth, we beseech Thee, O Lord, Thy grace into our hearts; that we, to
whom the incarnation of Christ, Thy Son, was made know by the message
of an angel, may by His Passion and Cross be brought to the glory of His
Resurrection, through the same Christ Our Lord.
Amen.

The Regina Caeli

— Said in place of the Angelus during the Easter Season

Queen of Heaven, rejoice, alleluia.
For He whom you did merit to bear, alleluia.
Has risen, as he said, alleluia.
Pray for us to God, alleluia.
Rejoice and be glad, O Virgin Mary, alleluia.
For the Lord has truly risen, alleluia.

Let us pray:
O God, who gave joy to the world through the resurrection of Thy Son, our
Lord Jesus Christ, grant we beseech Thee, that through the intercession of the
Virgin Mary, His Mother, we may obtain the joys of everlasting life. Through
the same Christ our Lord.
Amen

Night Prayer

1. EXAMINATION OF CONSCIENCE

The nightly examination of conscience should be brief, lasting
2-3 minutes. It is based on three simple questions:
- Where did I encounter God today?
- Where did I sin or reject God today?
- How will I live in closer union with God tomorrow?

2. THE MAGNIFICAT
— *Recited in the Divine Office in Evening Prayer (Luke 1:46-55)*

My soul magnifies the Lord,
and my spirit rejoices in God my Savior,
for he has regarded the low estate of his handmaiden.

For behold, henceforth all generations will call me blessed;
for he who is mighty has done great things for me,
and holy is his name.

And his mercy is on those who fear him
from generation to generation.

He has shown strength with his arm,
he has scattered the proud in the imagination of their hearts,
he has put down the mighty from their thrones,
and exalted those of low degree;
he has filled the hungry with good things,
and the rich he has sent empty away.

He has helped his servant Israel,
in remembrance of his mercy,
as he spoke to our fathers,
to Abraham and to his posterity forever.
Amen.

Recite the Most Holy Rosary of the Blessed Virgin Mary

Shortly after the Great Jubilee, Pope St. John Paul II charted a course for the Church in the third millennium: "To contemplate the face of Christ, and to contemplate it with Mary, is the 'programme' which I have set before the Church at the dawn of the third millennium, summoning her to put out into the deep on the sea of history with the enthusiasm of the new evangelization" *(Pope St. John Paul II, Ecclesia de Eucaristia, #6).* Further, he made the Rosary an essential aspect of this "programme." "The Rosary ... represents a most effective means of fostering among the faithful that commitment to the contemplation of the Christian mystery which I have proposed in the Apostolic Letter *Novo Millennio Ineunte* as a genuine 'training in holiness' ... The Rosary, precisely because it starts with Mary's own experience, is an exquisitely contemplative prayer" *(Pope St. John Paul II, Rosarium Virginis Mariae, #5 and #12).*

Indeed, through the Rosary, Mary gives to us the treasures of her heart. She hands on to us her own contemplation of the life she lived with Christ: "His mother kept all these things in her heart" *(Luke 2:51).* As such, the Rosary is a key to unlock the mystery of the life that the Holy Family lived at Nazareth. This hidden life of the Holy Family at Nazareth is the school of authentic Christian life: "Nazareth is a kind of school where we may begin to discover what Christ's life was like and even to understand his Gospel ... Here everything speaks to us, everything has meaning ... How I would like to return to my childhood and attend the simple yet profound school that is Nazareth" *(Pope St. Paul VI, Address at the Basilica of the Annunciation, January 5, 1964).*

This link to the life of the Holy Family at Nazareth helps us to understand the statement of Pope St. Pius X: "The Rosary, of all prayers, is the most beautiful, the most rich in grace, the one which most touches the heart of the Mother of God. If you want peace to reign in your home, say the beads [i.e. Rosary] there, every day, with your family."

Through the Rosary, we ask Mary to lead us into the School at Nazareth so that we may learn its secrets; so that our family may be transformed; so that we may experience the promise of peace: "The revival of the Rosary in Christian families ... will be an effective aid to countering the devastating effects of this crisis typical of our age" *(Pope St. John Paul II, Rosarium Virginis Mariae, #6).*

See ws 47-66 for Scriptural passages and meditation starters.

Read Scripture Using Lectio Divina

The Scriptures are like no other books on earth: "Holy Mother Church ... holds that the books of both the Old and New Testaments in their entirety ... are sacred ... because written under the inspiration of the Holy Spirit, they have God as their author" *(Second Vatican Council, Dei Verbum, #11)*. As such, the Bible should be read like no other book: "Prayer should accompany the reading of Sacred Scripture, so that a dialogue takes place between God and man. For 'we speak to him when we pray; we listen to him when we read the divine oracles'" *(Catechism #2653)*.

The Church's time honored method for reading the Scriptures is *Lectio Divina* (the divine reading), which is composed of four parts:

LECTIO OR READING
- Gently read a passage of Scripture.
- When a thought, word or passage strikes you, pause to dwell on it, repeating it slowly.
- When the passage has "dried up," move on to the next passage.

MEDITATIO OR MEDITATION
- Dwell at leisure on a morsel of the text.
- Personalize the passage by asking, "What is God saying to ME through the passage?"
- Do not work hard, actively trying to "crack" the text.
- Listen and allow God to speak through the text.

ORATIO OR PRAYER
- Allow the Word of God to move from the lips to the heart so that there is a desire for the text to be "opened up."
- Pray for God to open the text for you: "Lord, that I might see" *(Luke 18:41)*.
- Ultimately, it is the desire for communion with God.

CONTEMPLATIO OR CONTEMPLATION
- The soul experiences God "speaking" or being "poured into" the soul.
- The soul cannot "force" the response of God. A moment of contemplation is God's initiative that must be received as a gift.
- The soul should linger as long as it perceives God's presence.

The Liturgy of the Table

God understands the importance of the dinner table! In the Old Testament, the Torah established the centrality of the dinner table in the life of Israel:

- The Kosher Laws virtually assured that Jewish families would eat dinner together.
- The Challah Laws required Jews to share their bread with others.
- The Paschal Sacrifice was eaten as a family meal, thereby uniting the dinner table with the Temple in Jerusalem.

In the New Testament, the dinner table was critical during the public ministry of Christ. In Christ's encounter with the disciples on the road to Emmaus on Easter Sunday, we can discover a template for the use of our own dinner table. It has four essential elements:

- **Accompaniment in daily life:** Christ walked with the disciples on their journey to Emmaus. "That very day two of them were going to a village named Emmaus, about seven miles from Jerusalem … Jesus himself drew near and went with them" *(Luke 24:13-15)*. We must be present to our family at dinner as the normal experience of the family.

- **Questions about everyday life:** During the walk, Christ asked the disciples about the things important in their life. "Jesus said to them, 'What is this conversation which you are holding with each other as you walk?'" *(Luke 24:17)*. While gathered with our families at the dinner table, we need to listen as they share about their normal everyday lives—which means we must turn off all other distractions.

- **The Word of God:** When the disciples reveal their struggles, Christ brought them clarity through the Word of God. "Beginning with Moses and all the prophets, Jesus interpreted to them in all the Scriptures the things concerning himself" *(Luke 24:27)*. We will find clarity to our struggles in the Scriptures.

- **The Discovery of God:** Jesus sat at table with the disciples and they discovered him in the "breaking of the bread" *(Luke 24:35)*. We need to help our family members discover Christ's presence. To do so, we should unite our tables more closely to the Church and the life of Christ made manifest in the liturgical calendar.

The Liturgy of the Table is one of the most powerful means of transforming the family.

The Practice of the Presence of God

All of our spiritual practices should have this goal. They lead us to live a life immersed in God: "In him we live and move and have our being" *(Acts 17:28)*. Within this context, one of the totally unique features of Christianity is that our God comes to us: "And the Word became flesh" *(John 1:14)*. Indeed, he abides within us: "If a man loves me, he will keep my word … and we will come to him and make our home with him" *(John 14:23)*. Our challenge is to find God dwelling within.

Brother Lawrence of the Resurrection, a 17th century Carmelite friar in Paris, has left us the perfect pathway. It is called the Practice of the Presence of God, which is:

- **The simplest practice:** You simply gently turn your attention to God, who is dwelling within. "I devote myself exclusively to remaining always in his holy presence. I keep myself in his presence by simple attentiveness and a general loving awareness of God that I call 'actual presence of God' or better, a quiet and secret conversation of the soul with God that is lasting" *(Practice of the Presence of God, p. 53)*.

- **The sweetest practice:** "Eye has not seen, nor ear heard, nor the heart of man conceived what God has prepared for those who love him" *(1 Corinthians 2:9)*. This was the experience of Brother Lawrence: "This sometimes results in interior, and often exterior, contentment and joys so great that I have to perform childish acts to control them and keep them from showing outwardly" *(Practice of the Presence of God, p. 53)*.

- **The most profound practice:** Since this exercise unites us to Christ—our supernatural end—it is to be preferred to all others. "A day in your courts is better than a thousand elsewhere" *(Psalm 84:10)*.

There are two important aids in the Practice of the Presence of God:

- **The Eucharist:** "He who eats my flesh and drinks my blood abides in me, and I in him" *(John 6:56)*.

- **Prayer Triggers:** Choose something repetitive in your day and establish it as a prayer trigger reminding you to unite yourself to God.

Making Time for God

"A 'what' without a 'when' is a 'never.'" We have now established the "what" of the spiritual life. Seven practices that can help you to live a life immersed in God ... provided that you actually work them ... and infuse them with the right spirit.

Now we must develop the "when" you are going to do these spiritual practices. The timing will obviously vary from person to person, but there are certain spiritual principles that will help you to develop a spiritual plan of life. First, we must recognize that "grace builds on nature." This means that we have a material body that must be cared for according to the laws of nature ... and we can frequently find a spiritual analogy to these natural laws. Here are the steps in developing a personalized Spiritual Plan of Life. Use these steps to fill out the 24-hour clock on the following page:

1. **Give Rest to Your Body – Give Rest to Your Soul**
   a. Sleep: Identify when you will get at least 7 hours of sleep per night.
   b. Leisure: Identify periods of relaxation in the day ... including having fun with your family.

2. **Feed Your Body – Feed Your Soul**
   a. Meals: Identify when you will eat 3 meals per day.
   b. Prayer: Identify the times for your morning, midday, evening and night prayers.

3. **Labor in the World – Labor in the Spiritual Life**
   a. Employment: Identify periods of work, including commute time.
   b. Lectio Divina: Identify time to read/study Scripture (most frequently with morning or night prayers).

For these exercises to truly transform your home into a "little Nazareth," you must suffuse all your spiritual practices with the spirit of Nazareth:

• **Abiding Presence:** You must work to find God in yourself and in your family members ... especially when you are gathered around the dinner table.
• **Joyful Service:** Do something to bring joy to each member of your family every week. Frequently, the greatest gift you can make is your time.
• **Loving Sacrifice:** On a daily basis, the greatest sacrifice frequently needed within the home is charity in speech: "If any one make no mistakes in what he says he is a perfect man" *(James 3:2)*.

This is the Spiritual Plan of My Life

12 am

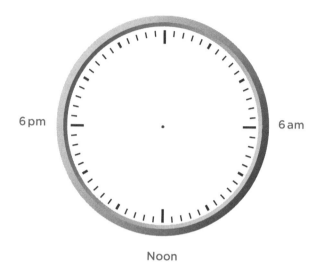

6 pm   6 am

Noon

Sleep:

Meals: *Breakfast:*
                  Lunch:
                  Dinner:

Prayer: *Morning:*
                  Daytime:
                  Night:

Work: *Morning:*
                  Afternoon:

Commute: *Morning:*
                  Afternoon:

Leisure/Open: *Before Dinner:*
                      After Dinner:

Our Lady and the New Springtime of Christianity

During the Great Jubilee, Pope St. John Paul II explicitly entrusted the Church's journey in the new millennium to Our Lady: "O Mother grant that ... the darkness will not prevail over the light. To you, Dawn of Salvation, we commit our journey through the new Millennium" *(October 8, 2000)*. In fact, Our Lady has been preparing the Church for this moment for the past 200 years. When Our Lady appeared in Paris, France in 1830 the Church entered into a "Marian era" *(Pope St. Paul VI, Signum Magnum, #6)*. Three approved Marian apparitions in the past 200 years stand out as particularly significant:

Rue du Bac, Paris, France (1830): Our Lady appeared to St. Catherine Laboure on July 18, 1830 with a message of dire importance: "The cross will be treated with contempt; they will hurl it to the ground. Blood will flow; they will open up again the side of Our Lord." Nonetheless, she assured St. Catherine that abundant graces would be shed upon those who "come to the foot of the altar." Our Lady returned on November 27, 1830 and gave to St. Catherine the image of the Miraculous Medal and promised: "All who wear it will receive great graces."

Lourdes, France (1858): Our Lady appeared to St. Bernadette Soubirous 18 times between February 11–July 16, 1858. On the apparition of February 25th, Mary revealed a hidden stream, which has been credited with countless healings. On March 25th she revealed her name: "I am the Immaculate Conception." Pope Pius XII declared Lourdes to be "an incomparable outpouring of the grace of redemption" *(Le Pelerinage de Lourdes, #10)*. Millions still flock to Lourdes every year.

Fatima, Portugal (1917): Mary appeared as Our Lady of the Rosary to three peasant children on the 13th of each month between May–October, 1917. Once more she had a message of dire importance: "God is about to punish the world for its crimes, by means of war, famine and persecutions of the Church and Holy Father." Nonetheless, she also had a message of great consolation: "In the end my Immaculate Heart will triumph ... and a period of peace will be granted to the world."

Lourdes and the Recovery of Desire

When Mary revealed the hidden stream to Bernadette on February 25, 1858, she said: "Go and drink at the fountain and wash yourself there!" This statement by Our Lady has two critical actions: to drink and to wash. Both are indispensable to the spiritual life and for families living in modern culture.

Desire is the fuel that drives our life. On the natural level, the brain's reward system places desires as goals to be attained. Once attained, the brain releases a dumping of dopamine to encourage the brain to repeat the action.

Desire is also the engine that drives our spiritual life. Christ reveals to us that desire is fuel that takes us all the way to heaven. Christ has been scourged beyond recognition. He has been nailed to a cross. Yet, his desire remains undimmed: "Jesus, knowing that all was now finished, said (to fulfill the scripture), 'I thirst'" *(John 19:28)*. Just moments before he dies, Christ reveals to us that he has an unsatiated desire for God. His love has not grown cold. Instead, it will pass through death to find fulfillment in heaven: "Love is strong as death" *(Song of Solomon 8:6)*.

Unfortunately, Satan has been manipulating humanity's desire from the beginning: "When the woman saw … that the tree was to be desired to make one wise, she took of its fruit and ate; and she also gave some to her husband, and he ate" *(Genesis 3:6)*. At this moment, love died in their hearts. They immediately hid themselves from God. Indeed, the beginning of trouble for humanity is the loss of love: "Repent and do the works you did at first" *(Revelation 2:5)*.

The men and women of our own time have certainly been hiding from God. Many have lost their thirst—not only for God, but also for each other. The love of many has grown cold. Indeed, many despair of ever finding or experiencing love. Our Lady came to Lourdes and revealed the hidden stream to help us recover our thirst: "Go and drink at the fountain." The healing of Lourdes is first and foremost a healing of the heart. Our Lady is willing to help with this healing even for those who cannot make it to Lourdes.

Lourdes and Immaculate Mary

The second critical action from Mary's statement: "Go and drink at the fountain and wash yourself there!" is to wash. Bernadette's own actions help us to better understand this request to wash.

When Our Lady asked Bernadette to drink and wash "at the fountain," Bernadette did not see a spring, so she headed to the Gave River. Our Lady stopped her and pointed to a little muddy path at the back of the grotto. Still not seeing a fountain, Bernadette began to scrape at the ground and then to smear the mud upon her face. The onlookers thought she was crazy. Lourdes almost came to an end that day. But later that night, the hidden stream became apparent and its waters became clear.

To understand the symbolism, we must return to the story of humanity's creation in the book of Genesis: "A mist went up from the earth ... then the Lord God formed man of dust from the ground, and breathed into his nostrils the breath of life" *(Genesis 2:6-7)*. A better translation than "dust" is "slime." When this slime is touched by the "breath of God," man becomes a living being.

Mary knows that the men and women of today need to experience a type of "re-creation." They must be washed from their sins and touched by God. Indeed, they must be touched by the merciful hand of God ... even as Mary was.

At Lourdes, Mary revealed her name, "I am the Immaculate Conception." In Catholic teaching, the Immaculate Conception is the greatest work of God's mercy. The mercy of God so fully enveloped Mary that Satan, sin and death had no power over her. This is the mercy that Mary wants the men and women of our day to experience—the merciful touch of God, which is why Lourdes represents "an incomparable outpouring of the grace of redemption."

At Lourdes, Mary helps us to trust in the mercy of God so that we can be "re-created" and rediscover our thirst for God. As such, Lourdes is a type of Paradise. Indeed, it is a type of Paradise where men and women may encounter the grace to live their marriages and family life as had been intended from the beginning.

"To Receive Mary into Your Home"
(Cf. John 19:27)

God has established Mary as an indispensable component of the Christian home. The Christian home was born when Joseph received Mary into his home *(Cf Matthew 1:24)*. In a certain sense, the Christian home passed to the Apostle John when he received Mary into his home *(Cf. John 19:27)*. It was Mary who opened the mystery of Nazareth to St. Charles de Foucauld, St. John Bosco, St.Therese and Pope St. John Paul II. Mary is also critical to your home. When you receive her into it, she will help transform it into "a little Nazareth."

Today, many people do not know Our Lady well and are concerned that devotion to Our Lady could rob Christ of his unique mediation: "There is one mediator between God and men ... Christ Jesus" *(1 Timothy 2:5)*.

To overcome these concerns and develop an authentic devotion to Our Lady, I suggest three actions. These actions will help deliver us from any scruple regarding devotion to Mary and help us to fulfill the vision she has brought to humanity in the past 200 years.

- **Ask Jesus to give you his love for his mother:** I began my relationship with Our Lady by standing in front of a picture of the Sacred Heart of Jesus and asking him for the grace to love his mother as he does. From that moment, love for Mary has continually increased in my heart. I have no scruples because I realize that my love for Mary pales in comparison to Christ's love for his mother.

- **Wear the Miraculous Medal around your neck:** At the beginning of the "Marian era," Our Lady promised great graces to those who wore the Miraculous Medal—especially around their neck. Wear a blessed Miraculous Medal around your neck every day.

- **Say the Rosary every day:** Mary appeared at Fatima as Our Lady of the Rosary and asked the children to say the Rosary every day. When we do, Mary opens to us the treasures of her heart, which was the life she shared with Jesus and St. Joseph at Nazareth. Indeed, through the Rosary, Mary helps to form our homes into an image of her home at Nazareth.

The Most Holy Rosary of the Blessed Virgin Mary

The Annunciation
Luke 1:26-38

"In the sixth month the angel Gabriel was sent from God to a city of Galilee named Nazareth, to a virgin betrothed to a man whose name was Joseph, of the house of David; and the virgin's name was Mary. And he came to her and said, 'Hail, O favored one, the Lord is with you!' But she was greatly troubled at the saying, and considered in her mind what sort of greeting this might be. And the angel said to her, 'Do not be afraid, Mary, for you have found favor with God. And behold, you will conceive in your womb and bear a son, and you shall call his name Jesus. He will be great, and will be called the Son of the Most High; and the Lord God will give to him the throne of his father David, and he will reign over the house of Jacob forever; and of his kingdom there will be no end.' And Mary said to the angel, 'How shall this be, since I have no husband?' And the angel said to her, 'The Holy Spirit will come upon you, and the power of the Most High will overshadow you; therefore the child to be born will be called holy, the Son of God. And behold, your kinswoman Elizabeth in her old age has also conceived a son; and this is the sixth month with her who was called barren. For with God nothing will be impossible.' And Mary said, 'Behold, I am the handmaid of the Lord; let it be to me according to your word.' And the angel departed from her."

MEDITATION STARTER

The first lesson in the School of Nazareth is humility or spiritual poverty. At the Annunciation, God's humility allows the Incarnation to be dependent upon the consent of Our Lady. In turn, Mary's "fiat" or "let it be to me" is the perfect example of "thy will be done" (Matthew 6:10). Humility is the entry point to an encounter with God. Let us pray for the humility to always say, "thy will be done" to God.

The Visitation
Luke 1:39-56

"In those days Mary arose and went with haste into the hill country, to a city of Judah, and she entered the house of Zechariah and greeted Elizabeth. And when Elizabeth heard the greeting of Mary, the babe leaped in her womb; and Elizabeth was filled with the Holy Spirit and she exclaimed with a loud cry, 'Blessed are you among women, and blessed is the fruit of your womb! And why is this granted me, that the mother of my Lord should come to me? For behold, when the voice of your greeting came to my ears, the babe in my womb leaped for joy. And blessed is she who believed that there would be a fulfilment of what was spoken to her from the Lord.' And Mary said, 'My soul magnifies the Lord, and my spirit rejoices in God my Savior, for he has regarded the low estate of his handmaiden. For behold, henceforth all generations will call me blessed; for he who is mighty has done great things for me, and holy is his name. And his mercy is on those who fear him from generation to generation. He has shown strength with his arm, he has scattered the proud in the imagination of their hearts, he has put down the mighty from their thrones, and exalted those of low degree; he has filled the hungry with good things, and the rich he has sent empty away. He has helped his servant Israel, in remembrance of his mercy, as he spoke to our fathers, to Abraham and to his posterity forever.' And Mary remained with her about three months, and returned to her home."

....

MEDITATION STARTER

The second lesson in the School of Nazareth is charity. As soon as Mary hears that Elizabeth is with child, she goes to be of assistance. Ultimately, Mary takes Christ abiding within her womb to Zechariah and Elizabeth. When the greeting of Mary reaches Elizabeth's ears, St. John the Baptist is sanctified in the womb! God wishes to use you to encounter others. Let us pray for the charity to bring Christ to those whom God places in our path.

The Nativity
Luke 2:1-19

"In those days a decree went out from Caesar Augustus that all the world should be enrolled ... And Joseph also went up from Galilee, from the city of Nazareth, to Judea, to the city of David, which is called Bethlehem, because he was of the house and lineage of David, to be enrolled with Mary, his betrothed, who was with child. And while they were there, the time came for her to be delivered. And she gave birth to her first-born son and wrapped him in swaddling cloths, and laid him in a manger, because there was no place for them in the inn. And in that region there were shepherds out in the field, keeping watch over their flock by night. And an angel of the Lord appeared to them, and ... said to them, 'Be not afraid ... for to you is born this day in the city of David a Savior, who is Christ the Lord. And this will be a sign for you: you will find a babe wrapped in swaddling cloths and lying in a manger.' And suddenly there was with the angel a multitude of the heavenly host praising God and saying, 'Glory to God in the highest, and on earth peace among men with whom he is pleased!' When the angels went away ... the shepherds said to one another, 'Let us go over to Bethlehem and see this thing that has happened ... ' And they went with haste, and found Mary and Joseph, and the babe lying in a manger. And ... Mary kept all these things, pondering them in her heart."

MEDITATION STARTER

The third lesson in the School of Nazareth is peace. It is the presence of Jesus Christ which brings peace. As such, the Holy Family experienced a heavenly peace on Christmas—even when cast out from "normal" lodgings. Indeed, to discover the presence of Christ, we must frequently separate ourselves from the hubbub of modern culture so that we can hear the "still, small voice" (1 Kings 19:12) of God. Let us pray for the grace to quiet external distractions so that we can focus upon Christ and experience his abiding peace.

The Presentation
Luke 2:21-39

"When the time came for their purification according to the law of Moses, they brought him up to Jerusalem to present him to the Lord ... and to offer a sacrifice according to what is said in the law of the Lord, 'a pair of turtledoves, or two young pigeons.' Now there was a man in Jerusalem, whose name was Simeon, and this man was righteous and devout, looking for the consolation of Israel, and the Holy Spirit was upon him. And it had been revealed to him by the Holy Spirit that he should not see death before he had seen the Lord's Christ. And inspired by the Spirit he came into the temple; and when the parents brought in the child Jesus ... he took him up in his arms and blessed God and said, 'Lord, now lettest thou thy servant depart in peace, according to thy word; for mine eyes have seen thy salvation which thou hast prepared in the presence of all peoples, a light for revelation to the Gentiles, and for glory to thy people Israel.' And his father and his mother marveled at what was said about him; and Simeon blessed them and said to Mary his mother, 'Behold, this child is set for the fall and rising of many in Israel, and for a sign that is spoken against (and a sword will pierce through your own soul also) that thoughts out of many hearts may be revealed' ... And when they had performed everything according to the law of the Lord, they returned into Galilee, to their own city, Nazareth."

....

MEDITATION STARTER

The fourth lesson in the School of Nazareth is the Cross. When we encounter Christ, he is always carrying his Cross. Simeon let Mary know that the Cross would always be part of her life. Let us pray for Mary's faith so that we may trust that whenever we experience the Cross of Christ, there will be the promise of his Resurrection.

The Finding in the Temple
Luke 2:41-52

"Now his parents went to Jerusalem every year at the feast of the Passover. And when he was twelve years old, they went up according to custom; and when the feast was ended, as they were returning, the boy Jesus stayed behind in Jerusalem. His parents did not know it, but supposing him to be in the company they went a day's journey, and they sought him among their kinsfolk and acquaintances; and when they did not find him, they returned to Jerusalem, seeking him. After three days they found him in the temple, sitting among the teachers, listening to them and asking them questions; and all who heard him were amazed at his understanding and his answers. And when they saw him they were astonished; and his mother said to him, 'Son, why have you treated us so? Behold, your father and I have been looking for you anxiously.' And he said to them, 'How is it that you sought me? Did you not know that I must be in my Father's house?' And they did not understand the saying which he spoke to them. And he went down with them and came to Nazareth, and was obedient to them; and his mother kept all these things in her heart. And Jesus increased in wisdom and in stature, and in favor with God and man."

MEDITATION STARTER

The fifth lesson in the School of Nazareth is prayer. "Mary kept all these things in her heart." This is the contemplative life ... lived in the home. Let us pray to embrace the vision of Pope St. John Paul II: "To contemplate the face of Christ, and to contemplate it with Mary, is the 'programme' which I have set before the Church at the dawn of the third millennium" (Pope St. John Paul II, Ecclesia de Eucharistia, #6).

The Baptism in the Jordan
Matthew 3:1-4:11

"In those days came John the Baptist, preaching in the wilderness of Judea, 'Repent, for the kingdom of heaven is at hand.' For this is he who was spoken of by the prophet Isaiah when he said, 'The voice of one crying in the wilderness: Prepare the way of the Lord' … Then Jesus came from Galilee to the Jordan to John, to be baptized by him … And when Jesus was baptized, he went up immediately from the water, and behold, the heavens were opened and he saw the Spirit of God descending like a dove, and alighting on him; and lo, a voice from heaven, saying, 'This is my beloved Son, with whom I am well pleased.' Then Jesus was led up by the Spirit into the wilderness to be tempted by the devil. And he fasted forty days and forty nights, and afterward he was hungry. And the tempter came and said to him, 'command these stones to become loaves of bread … throw yourself down [from the pinnacle of the temple] … fall down and worship me.' Then Jesus said to him, 'Begone, Satan! for it is written, 'You shall worship the Lord your God and him only shall you serve.' Then the devil left him, and behold, angels came and ministered to him."

....

MEDITATION STARTER

The sixth lesson in the School of Nazareth is the battle with evil. Immediately, after his baptism in the Jordan, Jesus is led by the Holy Spirit to battle Satan. The devil offers him the three fundamental temptations: the flesh, the world and the devil. Jesus won the battle in the desert … and he won the battle over Mary. By the grace of Christ, Satan never had access to Mary. Let us pray for the grace to be docile to the inspirations of the Holy Spirit so we may avoid temptation and embrace the will of God.

The Wedding Feast of Cana
John 2:1-11

"On the third day there was a marriage at Cana in Galilee, and the mother of Jesus was there; Jesus also was invited to the marriage, with his disciples. When the wine failed, the mother of Jesus said to him, 'They have no wine.' And Jesus said to her, 'O woman, what have you to do with me? My hour has not yet come. His mother said to the servants, 'Do whatever he tells you.' Now six stone jars were standing there, for the Jewish rites of purification, each holding twenty or thirty gallons. Jesus said to them, 'Fill the jars with water.' And they filled them up to the brim. He said to them, 'Now draw some out, and take it to the steward of the feast.' So they took it. When the steward of the feast tasted the water now become wine, and did not know where it came from (though the servants who had drawn the water knew), the steward of the feast called the bridegroom and said to him, 'Every man serves the good wine first; and when men have drunk freely, then the poor wine; but you have kept the good wine until now.' This, the first of his signs, Jesus did at Cana in Galilee, and manifested his glory; and his disciples believed in him."

MEDITATION STARTER

The seventh lesson in the School of Nazareth is the battle over the family. Immediately after withstanding Satan in the desert, Jesus Christ worked his first miracle by bringing superabundant joy back into the union of husband and wife. It was a small reflection of the joy of the Holy Family that was "a Paradise on earth" (Monsignor Jean Jacques Olier, Sentiments of M. Olier on The Devotion to St. Joseph). The Devil robbed husband and wife of joy in the Garden of Eden and seeks to do so unto today. "The family is placed at the heart of the great struggle between good and evil" (Pope St. John Paul II, Letter to Families, #23). Let us ask Our Lady to intercede with Christ so that our homes may experience superabundant joy.

The Transfiguration
Matthew 17:1-13

"And after six days Jesus took with him Peter and James and John his brother, and led them up a high mountain apart. And he was transfigured before them, and his face shone like the sun, and his garments became white as light. And behold, there appeared to them Moses and Elijah, talking with him. And Peter said to Jesus, 'Lord, it is well that we are here; if you wish, I will make three booths here, one for you and one for Moses and one for Elijah.' He was still speaking, when lo, a bright cloud overshadowed them, and a voice from the cloud said, 'This is my beloved Son, with whom I am well pleased; listen to him.' When the disciples heard this, they fell on their faces, and were filled with awe. But Jesus came and touched them, saying, 'Rise, and have no fear.' And when they lifted up their eyes, they saw no one but Jesus only. And as they were coming down the mountain, Jesus commanded them, 'Tell no one the vision, until the Son of man is raised from the dead.' And the disciples asked him, 'Then why do the scribes say that first Elijah must come?' He replied, Elijah does come, and he is to restore all things; but I tell you that Elijah has already come, and they did not know him, but did to him whatever they pleased. So also the Son of man will suffer at their hands.' Then the disciples understood that he was speaking to them of John the Baptist."

MEDITATION STARTER

The ninth lesson in the School of Nazareth is Christ's presence in the home. Mary and Joseph stood in awe of the Word Incarnate present in their home every day. When the apostles witnessed the divinity of Christ shining through his humanity, they were filled with "awe." "Husband and wife are called to be obedient to each other in the awe of Christ" (Ephesians 5:21). Spouses are called to so profoundly discover Christ's presence in their marriage that they are filled with awe. Let us pray for the grace to discover Christ so profoundly in our marriages that our homes truly become "ecclesia domestica"—the domestic church.

The Institution of the Most Holy Eucharist
Luke 22:1-23

"Now the feast of Unleavened Bread drew near ... Then Satan entered into Judas called Iscariot ... he went away and conferred with the chief priests and officers how he might betray him to them. And they were glad, and engaged to give him money ... Then came the day of Unleavened Bread, on which the Passover lamb had to be sacrificed ... And ... [Jesus] sat at table, and the apostles with him. And he said to them, 'I have earnestly desired to eat this Passover with you before I suffer; for I tell you I shall not eat it until it is fulfilled in the kingdom of God.' And he took a cup, and when he had given thanks he said, 'Take this, and divide it among yourselves; for I tell you that from now on I shall not drink of the fruit of the vine until the kingdom of God comes.' And he took bread, and when he had given thanks he broke it and gave it to them, saying, 'This is my body which is given for you. Do this in remembrance of me.' And likewise the cup after supper, saying, 'This cup which is poured out for you is the new covenant in my blood. But behold the hand of him who betrays me is with me on the table. For the Son of man goes as it has been determined; but woe to that man by whom he is betrayed!'"

....

MEDITATION STARTER

The tenth lesson in the School of Nazareth is the inseparable union between the Eucharist and the spousal union. The Word became Incarnate in Our Lady when she was "overshadowed" (Luke 1:35) by the Holy Spirit. The bread and wine are transformed into the Body, Blood, Soul and Divinity of Jesus Christ by the power of the Holy Spirit. Husband and wife are joined together in a sacramental union where Christ is present in their midst by the grace of the Holy Spirit. Marriage and the Eucharist are inseparably bound together. "In [the Eucharist] ... Christian spouses encounter the source from which their own marriage covenant flows, is interiorly structured and continuously renewed" (Pope St. John Paul II, Familiaris Consortio, #57). Let us pray for the grace to ever more profoundly unite our marriages and families to the Eucharist.

The Agony in the Garden
Luke 22:39-54

"Jesus came out, and went, as was his custom, to the Mount of Olives; and the disciples followed him. And when he came to the place he said to them, 'Pray that you may not enter into temptation.' And he withdrew from them about a stone's throw, and knelt down and prayed, 'Father, if thou art willing, remove this cup from me; nevertheless, not my will, but thine, be done.' And there appeared to him an angel from heaven, strengthening him. And being in an agony he prayed more earnestly; and his sweat became like great drops of blood falling down upon the ground. And when he rose from prayer, he came to the disciples and found them sleeping for sorrow, and he said to them, 'Why do you sleep? Rise and pray that you may not enter into temptation.' While he was still speaking, there came a crowd, and the man called Judas, one of the twelve, was leading them. He drew near to Jesus to kiss him; but Jesus said to him, 'Judas, would you betray the Son of man with a kiss?' And when those who were about him saw what would follow, they said, 'Lord, shall we strike with the sword?' And one of them struck the slave of the high priest and cut off his right ear. But Jesus said, 'No more of this!' And he touched his ear and healed him ... Then they seized Jesus and led him away, bringing him into the high priest's house."

MEDITATION STARTER

The eleventh lesson in the School of Nazareth is the self-emptying nature of love. At the Annunciation the Word emptied himself to take on a human nature. In the Agony in the Garden, Christ goes further and empties himself to accept "death, even death on a cross" (Philippians 2:8). At the Annunciation, the humility of God was met by the humility of Mary. Such will also be true at the foot of the Cross. Let us pray for the grace to be faithful to the demands of love.

The Scourging at the Pillar
John 18:28-19:1

"Then they led Jesus from the house of Caiaphas to the praetorium ... [and] Pilate went out to them and said, 'What accusation do you bring against this man? ... Take him yourselves and judge him by your own law.' The Jews said to him, 'It is not lawful for us to put any man to death' ... Pilate entered the praetorium again and called Jesus, and said to him, 'Are you the King of the Jews? ... Your own nation and the chief priests have handed you over to me; what have you done?' Jesus answered, 'My kingship is not of this world; if my kingship were of this world, my servants would fight, that I might not be handed over to the Jews; but my kingship is not from the world.' Pilate said to him, 'So you are a king?' Jesus answered, 'You say that I am a king. For this I was born, and for this I have come into the world, to bear witness to the truth. Everyone who is of the truth hears my voice.' Pilate said to him, 'What is truth? After he had said this, he went out to the Jews again, and told them, 'I find no crime in him. But you have a custom that I should release one man for you at the Passover; will you have me release for you the King of the Jews?' They cried out again, 'Not this man, but Barabbas!' Now Barabbas was a robber. Then Pilate took Jesus and scourged him."

MEDITATION STARTER

Lesson twelve in the School of Nazareth is love's willingness to serve. Christ let his apostles know that life in the kingdom looks radically different than life in the world: "Let the greatest among you become as the youngest, and the leader as one who serves" (Luke 22:26). This is the life he experienced in the home at Nazareth. Although Christ is God, he was obedient to Joseph and Mary. Although Mary is the Immaculate Conception, she allowed herself to be led by God working through St. Joseph. Let us pray for the grace to scourge the pride that seeks to be first so that we may truly serve our family on the way to salvation.

The Crowning of Thorns
John 19:2-16

"And the soldiers plaited a crown of thorns, and put it on Jesus' head, and arrayed him in a purple robe; they came up to him, saying, 'Hail, King of the Jews!' and struck him with their hands ... Jesus came out, wearing the crown of thorns and the purple robe. Pilate said to them, 'Behold the man!' The chief priests and the officers ... cried out, 'Crucify him, crucify him! ... We have a law, and by that law he ought to die, because he has made himself the Son of God.' When Pilate heard these words, he was the more afraid; he entered the praetorium again and said to Jesus, ... 'You will not speak to me? Do you not know that I have power to release you, and power to crucify you?' Jesus answered him, 'You would have no power over me unless it had been given you from above ...' Upon this Pilate sought to release him, but the Jews cried out, 'If you release this man, you are not Caesar's friend; everyone who makes himself a king sets himself against Caesar.' When Pilate heard these words, he brought Jesus out and sat down on the judgment seat at a place called The Pavement, and in Hebrew, Gabbatha. Now it was the day of Preparation of the Passover; it was about the sixth hour. He said to the Jews, 'Behold your King!' They cried out, 'Away with him, away with him, crucify him! ... We have no king but Caesar.' Then he handed him over to them to be crucified."

MEDITATION STARTER

The thirteenth lesson in the School of Nazareth is the interiority of the spiritual life. Mary and Joseph found Christ within their home. Outside of the home, they experienced tribulation. Likewise, when Pilate entered into the praetorium, he was alone with Jesus and had clarity of thought. When Pilate went outside, he was carried away by the desires of the crowd. Let us pray for the grace to have interiority in our spiritual lives—finding God within ourselves and within our homes. Then we will have clarity of thought.

The Carrying of the Cross
Luke 23:26-30; John 19:17-24

"As they led him away, they seized one Simon of Cyrene, who was coming in from the country, and laid on him the cross, to carry it behind Jesus. And there followed him a great multitude of the people, and of women who bewailed and lamented him. But Jesus turning to them said, 'Daughters of Jerusalem, do not weep for me, but weep for yourselves and for your children. For behold, the days are coming when they will say, 'Blessed are the barren, and the wombs that never bore, and the breasts that never nursed!' Then they will begin to say to the mountains, 'Fall on us'; and to the hills, 'Cover us.'" So they took Jesus, and he went out, bearing his own cross, to the place called the place of a skull, which is called in Hebrew Golgotha. There they crucified him, and with him two others, one on either side, and Jesus between them. Pilate also wrote a title and put it on the cross; it read, 'Jesus of Nazareth, the King of the Jews' ... When the soldiers had crucified Jesus they took his garments and made four parts, one for each soldier; also his tunic. But the tunic was without seam, woven from top to bottom; so they said to one another, 'Let us not tear it, but cast lots for it to see whose it shall be.' This was to fulfil the scripture, 'They parted my garments among them, and for my clothing they cast lots.'"

....

MEDITATION STARTER

The fourteenth lesson in the School of Nazareth is the communitarian nature of love. In the Garden of Eden, God said, "It is not good that the man should be alone" (Genesis 2:18). At the Annunciation, the Word chose to enter into a human family. On the way of the Cross, Christ had Simon of Cyrene to help him. God also wishes us to walk the spiritual journey together with others—beginning with our spouse and children. Let us pray for the grace to discern the people God is sending to accompany us on our spiritual journey.

The Crucifixion
John 19:17-35

"Standing by the cross of Jesus were his mother, and his mother's sister, Mary the wife of Clopas, and Mary Magdalene. When Jesus saw his mother, and the disciple whom he loved standing near, he said to his mother, 'Woman, behold, your son!' Then he said to the disciple, 'Behold, your mother!' And from that hour the disciple took her to his own home. After this Jesus, knowing that all was now finished, said (to fulfil the scripture), 'I thirst.' A bowl full of vinegar stood there; so they put a sponge full of the vinegar on hyssop and held it to his mouth. When Jesus had received the vinegar, he said, 'It is finished'; and he bowed his head and gave up his spirit. Since it was the day of Preparation, in order to prevent the bodies from remaining on the cross on the Sabbath ... the Jews asked Pilate that their legs might be broken, and that they might be taken away. So the soldiers came and broke the legs of the first, and of the other who had been crucified with him; but when they came to Jesus and saw that he was already dead, they did not break his legs. But one of the soldiers pierced his side with a spear, and at once there came out blood and water. He who saw it has borne witness—his testimony is true, and he knows that he tells the truth—that you also may believe."

MEDITATION STARTER

The fifteenth lesson in the School of Nazareth is that the love of God is manifested through others. Christ has an insatiable thirst for love. In the eyes of his mother, he can see the love that enveloped him from the moment of the Incarnation until his death upon the Cross. When Christ's heart was opened, he gave you a share in his insatiable thirst for love. Let us pray for the grace to see God's love enveloping us through the people he has placed in our life.

The Resurrection of Jesus
John 20:1-18

"Now on the first day of the week Mary Magdalene came to the tomb early, while it was still dark, and saw that the stone had been taken away from the tomb. So she ran, and went to Simon Peter and the other disciple, the one whom Jesus loved, and said to them, 'They have taken the Lord out of the tomb, and we do not know where they have laid him.' Peter then came out with the other disciple, and they went toward the tomb. They both ran, but the other disciple outran Peter and reached the tomb first; and stooping to look in, he saw the linen cloths lying there, but he did not go in. Then Simon Peter came, following him, and went into the tomb; he saw the linen cloths lying, and the napkin, which had been on his head, not lying with the linen cloths but rolled up in a place by itself. Then the other disciple, who reached the tomb first, also went in, and he saw and believed; for as yet they did not know the scripture, that he must rise from the dead. Then the disciples went back to their homes. But Mary stood weeping outside the tomb … she turned round and saw Jesus standing … Jesus said to her, 'Woman, why are you weeping? … Do not hold me, for I have not yet ascended to the Father; but go to my brethren' … Mary Magdalene went and said to the disciples, 'I have seen the Lord.'"

MEDITATION STARTER

The sixteenth lesson in the School of Nazareth is the eternal nature of love. It was impossible for death to hold Christ (Cf. Acts 2:24). "Love is strong as death" (Song of Solomon 8:6). When we are faithful to love, we will certainly experience tribulation. Nonetheless, the tribulation passes, but the love endures. We have received the assurance of a resurrection. Let us pray for the grace to believe more firmly in Christ's Resurrection so that we may be more faithful to the demands of love.

The Ascension into Heaven
Acts 1:1-11

"In the first book, O Theophilus, I have dealt with all that Jesus began to do and teach, until the day when he was taken up, after he had given commandment through the Holy Spirit to the apostles whom he had chosen. To them he presented himself alive after his passion by many proofs, appearing to them during forty days, and speaking of the kingdom of God. And while staying with them he charged them not to depart from Jerusalem, but to wait for the promise of the Father, which, he said, 'you heard from me, for John baptized with water, but before many days you shall be baptized with the Holy Spirit.' So when they had come together, they asked him, 'Lord, will you at this time restore the kingdom to Israel?' He said to them, 'It is not for you to know times or seasons which the Father has fixed by his own authority. But you shall receive power when the Holy Spirit has come upon you; and you shall be my witnesses in Jerusalem and in all Judea and Samaria and to the end of the earth.' And when he had said this, as they were looking on, he was lifted up, and a cloud took him out of their sight. And while they were gazing into heaven as he went, behold, two men stood by them in white robes, and said, 'Men of Galilee, why do you stand looking into heaven? This Jesus, who was taken up from you into heaven, will come in the same way as you saw him go into heaven.'"

....

MEDITATION STARTER

The seventeenth lesson in the School of Nazareth is that love unites us to God. "God is love" (1 John 4:16). As such, love is not bound by this world. Rather, it is the path leading to union with God. Christ has traveled this path before us. His Ascension gives us hope that our love will stretch all the way from this world to find union with God in the next. Let us pray for the grace to set our minds and hearts on our eternal destiny in heaven.

The Descent of the Holy Spirit
Acts 1:12-14; 2:1-11

"Then they returned to Jerusalem from the mount called Olivet, which is near Jerusalem, a Sabbath day's journey away; and when they had entered, they went up to the upper room, where they were staying, Peter and John and James and Andrew, Philip and Thomas, Bartholomew and Matthew, James the son of Alphaeus and Simon the Zealot and Judas the son of James. All these with one accord devoted themselves to prayer, together with the women and Mary the mother of Jesus, and with his brothers. When the day of Pentecost had come, they were all together in one place. And suddenly a sound came from heaven like the rush of a mighty wind, and it filled all the house where they were sitting. And there appeared to them tongues as of fire, distributed and resting on each one of them. And they were all filled with the Holy Spirit and began to speak in other tongues, as the Spirit gave them utterance. Now there were dwelling in Jerusalem Jews, devout men from every nation under heaven. And at this sound the multitude came together, and they were bewildered, because each one heard them speaking in his own language. And they were amazed and wondered, saying, 'Are not all these who are speaking Galileans? And how is it that we hear, each of us in his own native language ... them telling ... the mighty works of God.'"

....

MEDITATION STARTER

The eighteenth lesson in the School of Nazareth is the working of the Holy Spirit. The proper name of the Holy Spirit is Love (Cf. St. Thomas Aquinas, Summa Theologica, 1.37.1). At the Annunciation, the Holy Spirit overshadowed Mary so that God's Son could be enveloped in love. During the Nuptial Mass, the Holy Spirit unites the hearts of husband and wife so that Christ—sacramentally dwelling in the spousal union—may be enveloped in love. Let us pray that the Holy Spirit would strengthen us with might through the inner man (Cf. Ephesians 3:16) so that we would be faithful to the demands of love and experience Christ's presence in our midst.

The Assumption of the Blessed Virgin Mary

Pope Pius XII, Munificentissimus Deus, #44

"After we have poured forth prayers of supplication again and again to God, and have invoked the light of the Spirit of Truth, for the glory of Almighty God who has lavished his special affection upon the Virgin Mary, for the honor of her Son, the immortal King of the Ages and the Victor over sin and death, for the increase of the glory of that same august Mother, and for the joy and exultation of the entire Church; by the authority of our Lord Jesus Christ, of the Blessed Apostles Peter and Paul, and by our own authority, we pronounce, declare, and define it to be a divinely revealed dogma: that the Immaculate Mother of God, the ever Virgin Mary, having completed the course of her earthly life, was assumed body and soul into heavenly glory."

MEDITATION STARTER

The nineteenth lesson in the School of Nazareth is the Wedding Feast of the Lamb. The love that Christ and Mary shared could not be bound to this earth. Mary remained one with Christ from the moment of the Incarnation until the soldier's lance struck the final blow. She is now one with Christ in heaven. The love we share with our spouse will not end. It is destined to be opened to a new dimension—to the Wedding Feast of the Lamb. Let us pray to maintain a supernatural outlook on our marriages and family life.

The Coronation of the Blessed Virgin Mary as Queen of Heaven and Earth
Matthew 19:16-29

"Behold, one came up to Jesus, saying, 'Teacher, what good deed must I do, to have eternal life?' And Jesus said to him, 'Why do you ask me about what is good? One there is who is good. If you would enter life, keep the commandments.' He said to him, 'Which?' And Jesus said, 'You shall not kill, You shall not commit adultery, You shall not steal, You shall not bear false witness, Honor your father and mother, and, You shall love your neighbor as yourself.' The young man said to him, 'All these I have observed; what do I still lack?' Jesus said to him, 'If you would be perfect, go, sell what you possess and give to the poor, and you will have treasure in heaven; and come, follow me.' When the young man heard this he went away sorrowful; for he had great possessions. And Jesus said to his disciples, 'Truly, I say to you, it will be hard for a rich man to enter the kingdom of heaven … Then Peter said in reply, 'Lo, we have left everything and followed you. What then shall we have?' Jesus said to them, 'Truly, I say to you, in the new world, when the Son of man shall sit on his glorious throne, you who have followed me will also sit on twelve thrones, judging the twelve tribes of Israel. And every one who has left houses or brothers or sisters or father or mother or children or lands, for my name's sake, will receive a hundredfold, and inherit eternal life.'"

MEDITATION STARTER

The twentieth lesson in the School of Nazareth is the victory of love. Christ has promised thrones and a kingdom to those who remain faithful until the end. Ultimately, it is fidelity to love … to the unending gift of self … even in the most difficult circumstances. Here's the hidden pearl. God is love. When we love we are bound to God. The love endures. The difficulties pass. The home is the school of love where we learn these lessons.

Resources

The Chaplet of Divine Mercy

Pope St. John Paul II's last message to humanity related to Divine Mercy: "How much need the world has to understand and accept Divine Mercy. Lord … we believe in you and with confidence repeat to you today: Jesus, I trust in You, have mercy on us and on the whole world" *(April 3, 2005).*

Pope St. John Paul II was speaking of the Divine Mercy apparitions to St. Faustina Kowalska in Poland during the 1930's. During these apparitions, Christ gave to St. Faustina a devotion known as "The Chaplet of Divine Mercy." It is said using the Rosary and takes less than 10 minutes. Christ requested for the Chaplet to be said between 3pm-4pm, when possible.

PRAYERS OF THE CHAPLET OF DIVINE MERCY: USING A ROSARY

1. Make the sign of the Cross. Say one Our Father, one Hail Mary and the Apostles Creed.
2. Beginning on the Our Father bead next to the medal, say one "Eternal Father" and ten "For the sake of His sorrowful Passion" prayers. (Repeat 5 times.)
3. Say three "Holy God" and "O Blood and Water" prayers.
4. Optional Prayer: "Eternal God, in whom mercy is endless and the treasury of compassion in exhaustible, look kindly upon us and increase Your mercy in us, that in difficult moments we might not despair nor become despondent, but with great confidence submit ourselves to Your holy will, which is Love and Mercy itself."
5. Close: Make the sign of the Cross.

ETERNAL FATHER

"Eternal Father, I offer You the Body and Blood, Soul and Divinity of Thy dearly beloved Son, Our Lord Jesus Christ, in atonement for our sins and those of the whole world."

FOR THE SAKE OF HIS SORROWFUL PASSION

"For the sake of His sorrowful Passion, have mercy on us and on the whole world."

HOLY GOD

"Holy God, Holy Mighty One, Holy Immortal One, have mercy on us and on the whole world."

O BLOOD AND WATER

"O Blood and Water which gushed forth from the Heart of Jesus as a fountain of mercy us, I trust in You."

How to Pray the Rosary

DETERMINE WHICH SET OF MYSTERIES YOU WILL PRAY

Joyful
Pray on Mondays and Saturdays

1st: The Annunciation
2nd: The Visitation
3rd: The Nativity of Our Lord
4th: The Presentation of Jesus in the Temple
5th: The Finding of Jesus in the Temple

Sorrowful
Pray on Tuesdays and Fridays

1st: The Agony in the Garden
2nd: The Scourging at the Pillar
3rd: The Crowning with Thorns
4th: The Carrying of the Cross
5th: The Crucifixion

Glorious
Pray on Wednesdays and Sundays

1st: The Resurrection of Our Lord
2nd: The Ascension of Our Lord
3rd: The Descent of the Holy Spirit
4th: The Assumption of Mary into Heaven
5th: The Crowning of Our Lady Queen of Heaven

Luminous
Pray on Thursdays

1st: The Baptism of Christ in the Jordan
2nd: The Wedding Feast at Cana
3rd: The Proclamation of the Kingdom
4th: The Transfiguration
5th: The Institution of the Eucharist

PRAY THE ROSARY

1 Make the Sign of the Cross and Pray the Apostles Creed.

2 Pray the Our Father.

3 Pray three Hail Marys for an increase in the virtues of faith, hope, and charity, followed by a Glory Be and Fatima Prayer.

4 Meditate on the First Mystery, praying the Our Father and ten Hail Marys using the 10 beads. Conclude the decade with the Glory Be and Fatima Prayer.

5 Repeat step 4 for each of the 5 mysteries of the Rosary.

6 Recite the concluding prayers, Hail Holy Queen and The Rosary Prayer, after praying the 5th mystery.

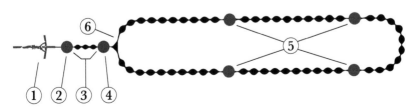

Prayers of the Rosary

THE APOSTLES CREED

I believe in God, the Father almighty, Creator of heaven and earth. I believe in Jesus Christ, His only Son, our Lord. He was conceived by the power of the Holy Spirit and born of the Virgin Mary. He suffered under Pontius Pilate, was crucified, died, and was buried. He descended to the dead. On the third day He rose again. He ascended into heaven, and is seated at the right hand of the Father. He will come again to judge the living and the dead. I believe in the Holy Spirit, the Holy Catholic Church, the communion of saints, the forgiveness of sins, the resurrection of the body, and life everlasting. Amen.

DECADE

OUR FATHER

Our Father, who art in heaven, hallowed be Thy name. Thy kingdom come; Thy will be done on earth as it is in heaven. Give us this day our daily bread; and forgive us our trespasses as we forgive those who trespass against us; and lead us not into temptation, but deliver us from evil. Amen.

GLORY BE

Glory be to the Father, and to the Son, and to the Holy Spirit; as it was in the beginning, is now, and ever shall be, world without end. Amen.

HAIL MARY x10

Hail Mary, full of grace, the Lord is with thee; blessed art thou among women, and blessed is the fruit of thy womb, Jesus. Holy Mary, Mother of God, pray for us sinners now and at the hour of our death. Amen.

FATIMA PRAYER

O my Jesus, forgive us our sins, save us from the fires of hell, and lead all souls to heaven, especially those most in need of Thy mercy.

HAIL HOLY QUEEN

Hail, holy Queen, mother of mercy, our life, our sweetness, and our hope. To thee do we cry, poor banished children of Eve; to thee do we send up our sighs, mourning and weeping in this valley of tears. Turn, then, most gracious advocate, thine eyes of mercy toward us; and after this, our exile, show unto us the blessed fruit of thy womb, Jesus. O clement, O loving, O sweet Virgin Mary.

V. Pray for us, O holy Mother of God.
R. That we may be made worthy of the promises of Christ.

THE ROSARY PRAYER

O God, whose only begotten Son, by His life, death, and resurrection has purchased for us the rewards of eternal life, grant, we beseech Thee, that meditating upon these mysteries of the most Holy Rosary of the Blessed Virgin Mary, we may imitate what they contain, and obtain what they promise, through the same Christ our Lord. Amen.

The Daily Plan of Life

1. MORNING PRAYER
- Consecration to Our Lady
- Protection Prayer
- Canticle of Zechariah (Benedictus)
- Paradisus Dei's Prayer for the New Evangelization

2. MIDDAY PRAYER
- Angelus or Regina Caeli

3. NIGHT PRAYER
- Examination of Conscience
- Canticle of Mary (Magnificat)

4. PRAY THE ROSARY

5. READING SCRIPTURE USING LECTIO DIVINA

6. LITURGY OF THE DINNER TABLE

7. PRACTICE OF THE PRESENCE OF GOD

Made in the USA
Middletown, DE
05 March 2024

50818554R00042